The SON-IN-LAW from SINDH

PREMILLA RAJAN

Copyright © Premilla Rajan 2025
All Rights Reserved.

ISBN
Paperback 979-8-89632-976-3
Hardcase 979-8-89744-671-1

Contents

Contents

About the book

The "Son-in-Law from Sindh" delves into the intricate cultural tapestry of the Bhaibund community of Sindh, a vibrant, resilient people whose stories are largely untold. Set against a backdrop of undivided India, this book traces families' journeys as they navigate the complex landscapes of identity, migration, and assimilation.

From the bustling streets of Hyderabad and Karachi to the colourful enclaves of Singapore and Malaysia, this brings to life a world where family bonds, societal expectations, and rich cultural heritage shape every choice. Through the experiences of a couple bound by love yet, challenged by the community's expectations, "Son-in-Law from Sindh" captures both the beauty and struggle of preserving one's roots while adapting to new surroundings.

This story concerns resilience, love, and the enduring ties connecting a scattered community across generations and continents.

In the twilight of his life, the protagonist grapples with his memories. It was a slow, heartbreaking loss, each slipping away like grains of sand. Diagnosed with dementia, he faces the tragic toll of past traumas and experiences that have worn down his resilience. Yet, amidst the shadows of forgetfulness, one light remains steady: the love that binds him to his family. This tender and unwavering relationship becomes his anchor, helping to sustain cherished bonds and connect him to his past, even as it fades. Through the support and patience of his wife and loved ones, he finds moments of clarity, allowing the enduring power of love to shine through the darkest moments of his journey.

A loner with previous marriages under his belt, at last, finds peace and solace with his Tamilian Brahmin wife, who is highly educated and poles apart in every which way!

A Marriage that has endured 18 years helps to stabilise the fractured nuances of his Life. As he often says, " ACK - Aur kya Chahiye!"

As a Seannachie, I consider it an honour to record the nuances of his saga in this book!

Foreword

To write the foreward for a book by Premilla Rajan is a rare honour for a modest writer like me. I have known Premilla for almost a decade and have been an avid admirer of her literary prowess. Through her debut work, *80 Wondrous Years* that she penned after turning an octogenarian, she took us through the remarkable saga of her life as a sprightly youth, dedicated army wife, caring parent and grandparent, eminent educationalist and bountiful philanthropist. Later, her versatility stood highlighted when she traversed the world of Hindu temples through a travelogue, *Sacred Trysts*, in a passionate attempt to inculcate some traditional Indian values in Gen Z. I am sure this latest work of hers, which not only manifests her compassion and modernistic outlook but also projects her scholarly acumen, would prove a page-turner.

I wish the book every success.

Capt. D P Ramachandran

War Veteran & Military Historian
Founder & Managing Trustee – Colours of Glory Foundation

Appreciation

"The Son-in-Law from Sindh" beautifully captures the intersection of love, identity, and cultural heritage across generations and continents. A poignant exploration of resilience, family bonds, and the enduring power of love amidst life's most challenging trials."

Dr. Arun Krishnan, PhD, MBA, Engineer, IT Bioinformatics, Computational Biology, HR Analytics.

Entrepeneur, Polyglot, Amateur musician, excelling in Guitar and percussion instruments, now an Author, of a brilliant Trilogy "The Battle of Vatapi."

Preface

We first met our son-in-law, Kishore Shewaram Mohinani, a Sindhi from the original undivided India, Hyderabad, Sindh, during a family holiday in 2005 in Sri Lanka.

It was the year soon after the horrible tsunami that had hit Sri Lanka and Galle in particular. There was devastation around, similar to the upheaval in Gayti's life 5 years earlier, almost mirroring the tragic aftermath of the divorce.

Gayti had arranged two beautiful villas, on the seashore, for 17 of us, including all the little ones! Gayti simply took charge, picking up the pieces with all our support.

My sister's family included Dhir, Sashi, Nikka, Raghav, and his friend from the states.

Kannan and I were joined by our children, Gayti and her two girls, Aisha and Rushi, our son, Harsh and Nimmi, and their little kids, Mandira and Anoushka.

We stayed in a lovely, charming Villa, "Sanda Kirana" or "Moon Beams"!

The second Villa hosted Gayti and her daughters along with Kishore, who was courting Gayti, Raghav, Nikka, and Raghav's friend.

A fun-filled atmosphere infused the family, and we enjoyed great evenings of togetherness, joy, and lovely games that reduced us to boisterous laughter and gay camaraderie, especially when we played dumb charades. Every evening was a family bonding and had crazy inventive drinks and games. I often wonder how Kishore took all those boisterous Tam Bram jokes. A sport that he is, he simply accepted the mood and went along!

Dhir and I were voted the worst actors possible!

The villas were located on the seashore; we strolled down to the sparkling sands each morning and walked straight into the shallows. The little ones squealed in joy as Harsh hoisted them on his shoulders while the waves tickled their feet.

At even time, magical moments were spent under the canopy of stars, sundowners in hand, munching happily on our delicious snacks from Chennai, as we watched distant ships navigate the ocean, with a twinkle of lights blinking at a distance!

Daily swims in the pool inside the villa gardens were another treat; With excellent service, we had a leisurely, carefree holiday with great fun and merriment.

I recall that the cuisine was fabulous, and the villa caretakers went overboard with the variety of Sri Lankan specialities served in 'propah' British style every morning!

The exquisite layout of exotic table mats and napkins would herald new beginnings, new gustatory pleasures, new plans of action, and visits!

Indeed, that holiday was memorable in more than one way. On the penultimate evening, with all of us around the huge bonfire, Kishore dropped to his knees to propose to Gayti!

We, as parents, had no clue about Kishore and his background.

Readers will be happy to note that the foundation for a strong bond of affection, friendship, and love, had just knitted the Rajan and the Mohinani families.

As we looked forward, Kannan and I decided to go South from Galle to KadiraGama to thank the Lord for these new developments in our child's life. Kadiragama houses a simple painted picture of Lord Muruga instead of an idol in the Sanctum, which was a religious influence from India years ago. The temple is a marvel, neat and clean, and the offerings are arranged in the most artistic aesthetic manner. Devotees can pick up a plate of offerings from the impeccable array on display!

We all met up again briefly in Colombo. As the rest of the party bid farewell and flew back to Hong Kong, Singapore, and Chennai; Kannan and I continued northward to explore Kandy and other exciting places in Sri Lanka. However, LTTE trouble shorted our foray further North to Ashoka Vana and Nuwara Eliya.

Gayti and her girls were based in Hong Kong. Her focus was empowering herself with added qualifications as a teacher for children with 'Special Needs'. Already a postgraduate in English Literature, she enrolled in the University of Hong Kong for her Post Graduate Diploma in Education and further qualifications from the UK to allow her to specialise in Special Needs Education. Aishwarya was on the verge of completing her A levels while Urvashi was in high school when Gayti decided to apply to Singapore for permanent residency for herself and the girls. The romance had rekindled her hopes. The Divorce had given her such a measure of self-confidence that she chose to be independent henceforth. She was granted PR for herself and her girls as a well-qualified teacher. That's how she came to Singapore!

Kishore and Gayti chose to rent an apartment in Nanak Mansions. It was a lovely duplex with winding stairs to the bedrooms on the first floor. From the large, spacious living and dining rooms, kitchen, powder room, and maid's quarters on the ground floor, huge French windows opened onto the lush lawns, the Tennis courts, and the swimming pool.

Dopey's space was under the stairs. It was in this charming place that Kishore and Gayti were wed.

As per Singapore Law, a Justice of Peace officiated at the wedding in 2008.

The bride and groom had written their vows independently and read them out.

The simple decor of gorgeous orchids and a Marquee on the lawns, a gathering of very close friends and family, a sumptuous dinner catered, and an evening of dance and merriment kept us in great spirits.

Our prayers and good wishes for the new couple were fervent. The following day, the family was at the beautiful Selva Vinayagar Kovil (established by Sri Lankans) to complete the ceremonies in the Tam Bram way of worship at the Kovil.

Aisha and Rushi, on the cusp of their 20s, perhaps had mixed emotions, as did we, too. We hoped that Gayti and Kishore would be happy with each other and that life would treat them gently, as both were divorced and had children to care for. Kishore was welcomed as a dear member of the family.

It has been nearly 18 years since our Singaporean Son-in-law became a valuable addition to the TamBram family from Old Madras, now known as Chennai! Thus, the connections to Tanjore and Trichy of Tamil Nadu began with the blessings of the Divine.

Welcoming my son-in-law from a different cultural background has been a wonderment. As we unravel his tangled past, we realise what Kishore once had all that in reality!

As he states charmingly that he was perhaps conceived in Sindh and birthed at Pune, (as the family had fled, just before the partition), avoiding the terrible holocaust that ensued in 1947! He grew up in Pune till he was 5 years old and then came to Singapore and ....

Ah! But I do run along gentle readers.......It is time to go down the wormhole of time, to Sindh of undivided India.

Part 1

Sindh

Chapter 1

Heritage of Sindh ...

One rarely finds a unique connection between history and heritage, dating back to 3000 BC. I found this strange connection during my stay in Singapore when I visited my daughter and son-in-law on a visit pass.

I stumbled upon it by remarkable coincidence because a significant population of Indians is in the Sindhi diaspora in Singapore.

"The Son-in-law from Sind", is an exploration of the antecedents of this unique community.

Inspiration came by as I had just finished reading Vineet Bajpai's 'Trilogy', which traces a part of the Harappan civilisation.

Further, Sindh was once part of undivided India and held a prominent place around 3000 BC as a rich cultural civilisation on the banks of Sindhu / Saraswati, part of the great Sapta Sindhu, or the seven rivers. We know the great Indus River, which irrigates large tracts of Punjab-Bharat and Pakistan through its five tributaries.

Come join me in exploring those times to the distant past of Sindh and its people ……

1. A Peep into the Past

We are often unaware of our past. There are secrets in the past that only interested and illustrious researchers stumble upon.

A look at the diverse historical events that shaped Sindh, including Empires, trades, and migrations that left an indelible mark on this region.

One such historian lived in Uttar Pradesh, and he wrote extensively about the history of Sindh:

Tareekh-e-Sindh (A History of Sindh), by Abdulhalim Sharar,(1860-1926).

Abdulhalim Sharar was born and lived much of his life in Uttar Pradesh. He was a prolific writer who produced biographies, romances, essays, historical novels, and more. The Tareekh-e-Sindh is considered to be his major historical work.

According to this book, the first permanent settlement in Sindh dates back to 7000 BC.

The Indus Valley civilisation, one of the world's oldest cultures, flourished between 3300 and 1750 BC, rivalling those of Egypt and Mesopotamia in size and sophistication. Sindh became a Persian province in the sixth century and was conquered by Alexander the Great in 326 BC. In the ensuing years, Buddhists, Greco-Bactrians, Scythians, and Persian Rajputs all held sway.

2. Geographical boundaries

Over centuries, Muslim geographers, historians, and travellers have called the entire region from the Arabian Sea to the Hindu Kush mountains Sindh.

An exploration reveals the distinct borders and natural terrain that shaped the place, people and culture.

The importance of the river Sindhu and the close resemblance in the nomenclature would perhaps make us consider Sindh an abbreviated form of Sindhu, the probable origin; Later, perhaps the phonetical changes turned Sindhu into Hindu in Pehlavi, as the Iranian influence was then prevalent. The Hebrews however, called it Hoddu.

While we marvel at the details of the past, it is essential to understand that other areas often border landlocked areas. Those usually influenced areas are termed geographical boundaries, and they determine the profound impact on adjoining areas.

Sindh is the province of south-eastern Pakistan presently, with Rajasthan and Gujarat at its Eastern borders. Sindh also boasts a coastline that goes to the Arabian Sea in the South.

The major cities are Hyderabad and Karachi, which are in the southern part of the province.

3. Historical influences

Let us see how the various historical events spawned Sindh's unique History and Culture.

Historically, Sindh was the site of one of the cradle civilisations, especially the Bronze Age Indus Valley civilisation; evidence points to the fabulous cities of ancient Mohenjodaro and the Malki Necropolis, now proclaimed UNESCO World Heritage sites.

However, the civilisation declined around 1000 BC as migrations overran the region. It is believed that the migrating tribes propagated the Iron Age that lasted till 500 BC.

It is said that the Vedas were composed during this period. The Vedas are indeed the most venerated Hindu scriptures, valued even today. In 518 BC, the Achaemenid empire conquered the Indus Valley and established the Hindu Kush Satrap in Sindh.

Then came Alexander the Great's invasion in 326 BC, after which Sindh became part of the Mauryan Empire.

After the decline of this Empire, the Indo-Greeks, Indo-Scythians, and Indo-Parthians ruled over Sindh.

Sindh is also known as 'Bab-ul-Islam', or 'Gateway to Islam' because it was one of the first regions of the Indian subcontinent to fall under Islamic rule.

History entails that in 711 BC, Ummayad general Muhamed bin Qasim conquered Sindh with 20,000 Cavalry and five catapults! This Arab conquest was followed by widespread conversion to Islam. Mansura was made the capital, and the port city of Debal was created.

Though the Rashidun had made early Muslim conquests, Islamisation began only after the Arab invasion by the Ummayed Caliphate under Muhammad bin Qasim in 711 BC. Several dynasties, including Habarris, Simran, Sammas, Arghuns, and Tarakhans, held sway in Sindh.

The Mughal Empire conquered Sindh in 1591 AD and organised it as 'Subha of Thatta', the first Imperial division. However, the Kalhora dynasty that came later conferred Independence. My research revealed an interesting fact: the Delta regions were often called 'Thattas'.

The British conquered Sindh only in 1843 AD after the battle of Hyderabad and gained Sindh from the Talpur Dynasty.

In 1936, Sindh became a separate province and part of Pakistan after Independence.

It is very interesting to note that in the ensuing centuries, the profound influences of the Greeks, Bactrians, Buddhists, Scythians, Persians, and Rajputs have contributed enormously and superimposed their traditions, on the original culture of the land.

(Historical input excerpts courtesy Wikipedia).

4. Original traditions

Going back in time, we understand how the comings and goings from the various borders would have affected the shades of cultural traditions, patterns of speech, cultural routines, the introduction of new traditions and norms, and other simple adaptations to the life that the original Sindhis led. A glimpse of the ancient traditions and folk practices, unique customs, that still resonate in the Community!

Though built around a beautiful river, the river valley civilisation needed to be sustained, and early Sindhis felt that the men needed to venture out of their borders to begin a trade or learn new trades and bring home the money to feed the wife and the children left behind.

Thus a tradition of Matriarchal society led by the senior most female member, generally the grandmother, would hold the reins; sustaining and preserving a culture where the youngsters were groomed strictly by women till the age of 17 years; then they would be apprenticed to their uncles or their fathers or their cousins in whatever business or trade that the family engaged in. This was referred to as 'Sindhiwarki' or 'Sindhiworki'.

Every two or three years, the young men returned to spend time with the family; the trip was also referred to as 'Musafiri', which meant a reunion with siblings and parents. Perhaps marriages were made then, and children were born during Musafiri.

Young men grew up under uncles or family members based elsewhere, absorbing values from them and imbibing new ideas and values of their new environment. Both cultural and economic practices from their new habitats thus influenced their ways of thinking. This was specific to the trading 'Sindhis or Bhaibands'.

This was the way of life they promoted; where the idea of passing on the norms of business traditions was well within a family.

This does hark back to the 'guild practices' that were perhaps in vogue in Western countries around those times. Sindh seemed to echo a similar tradition, and youngsters opted out of regular schooling, for a more hands-on approach to their thriving businesses, initially started by their parents, the men folk, their cousins, uncles, and so on.

This practice continued well into the 20th century.

Remarkably, the continuous invasions of the region perhaps helped disperse the men folk to the West and the East. That is why even today we find Sindhis spread all over the world.

It was expected to find youngsters married off in their teens before they ventured out!

Further, the matriarchs also accepted having another wife and children in another country and place of work.

Strangely, children's names were often repeated in the new family setup!! Some of Kishore's cousins in the Philippines have the names of their stepbrothers and sisters left behind at Sindh or Pune!!

5. The Language

The Sindhi language is said to be derived from Sanskrit and is closely related to ancient Prakrit. Due to its geographical isolation, Sindh developed its unique vocabulary, though it has heavily borrowed from Punjab, Gujarat, and Rajasthan. A smattering of Urdu has also trickled in.

The language that the people used to communicate was a vernacular version of Prakrit, an Indo-Aryan language that was prevalent from the third century BC to about the eighth century.

The written versions, however, came into being only around the eighth century CE.

The very first writing was the translation of the Quran in the eighth century.

Fascinating indeed, is the fact that written Sindhi emerged only in the 11th century.

It is to the credit of three Sufi mystics and poets-Qad-i-Qadan-(1463-1551), Shah Abdul Karim (1536-1623) and Shah Inat Rizvi of the late 17th century who helped Sindhi literature acquire form and structure.

The Sindhi language's ability to blend the features of Islamic works with Hindu Vedic texts and the tenets of Sikhism speaks of a high degree of Inclusion in faith and beliefs and acceptance.

Treatises were also written in Sindhi, Astronomy, Medicine, and History in the eighth and ninth centuries.

Thus the language itself is rather ancient, with a rich literature to boast of, both in prose and poetry. It is said that Sindhi poets often recited before the Muslim Caliphs of Baghdad.

However, as we have seen earlier, the borders profoundly influenced spoken dialects. Hence, there are differences between those in the north of Sindh and those in the South.

The Sindhi language has many dialects and forms a direct continuum with neighbouring languages such as Gujarati and Saraiki.

Each area of Sindh has a different dialect with its script! However, the dialect identifies the location, too, making it easily recognisable to the population.

The script adopted is Perso-Arabic with new letters adapted to the phonology; differing from Urdu which has a more Arabic version. Both scripts move from right to left.

In the 15th century, the Sindhi script was standardised, and 'Devanagari' was adopted for trading. 'Landa', a form of 'Gurmukhi', was used for literary and religious purposes.

Finally, in the 19th century, the Perso-Arabic script was decreed standard over the Devanagari script.

Interestingly, the Khudabadi script of 1550 CE was used by the Hindu community till the colonial era.

Today, the Sindhi Roman script is widely used in mobile communication!

Readers interested in language development in Sindh are encouraged to search the Internet, notably Wikipedia, for a treasure trove of details.

For our story the information shared is adequate.

(Inputs on language details are courtesy of several authors who have touched upon this aspect in their various articles from the National Library of Singapore).

6. Religion

This section examines religious diversity, focusing on the peaceful coexistence of various faiths and how these shaped the region's moral and social fabric.

Sindhis are Hindus, Sikhs, Muslims & Christians by faith and are wonderfully tolerant.

The advent of Islamic invaders brought the Islamic faith, and later, Colonial powers brought in Christianity.

The proximity of Punjab allowed Sikhism to be a natural addition to the original Hindu population.

Sindhis do not have a defined Caste system; however, they subscribe to 'Zaats' associated with certain distinct cultural and behavioural characteristics. One of the oldest tribes is Charan, which is said to have existed since 7000 BC.

90% of the population is Hindu, and Sikhs form 10%. The Culture of Sufism penetrated the Hindu tenets.

Hindus worshipped the River Sindhu, Varuna the Water God and Jhulelal.

Jhulelal was referred to as 'Lal Ahahbaz Qalandar' (1177-1278) of the mystic Suhrawady Sufi order and was also referred to as Kizier or Sheik Tazir. However, this was not popular for several hundred years thereafter.

Life and story of Jhulelal

'Jhulelal the God of Water, God of the Indus' [Sindhu river].

Courtesy Sindiyat.org and excerpts from the book 'Sindhiyat' by Thulsidas Ahuja.

(National Library Singapore).

As earlier said, the region of Sindh was prosperous on all fronts—culture, heritage, wealth, and Spiritual value. It was the land where Vedas were brought home to the people as early as the 8th century!

People were generally peaceful and happy. As we glean from History, Greed and the Aggrandisement of the neighbours induced the invasions by foreigners.

Their provinces or Thattas were taken over by one Mirkshah - a man known for his tyrannical disposition and total fanaticism.

Advised by his courtiers he was persuaded by them to use his power to convert the people to Islam, as a means to attaining Jannat or Heaven!

So it is said that Mirkshah issued the 'Shaahi Farmaan', or Royal decree, which simply ordered conversion or death!

The Hindus were overwhelmed and sought help from the only Gods they knew: Varuna, the Water God, and their beloved River!

Their chieftain or Mukhi bargained for time with the Shah, and the Hindus bravely congregated on the banks of the Sindhu to offer penance and oblation as worship for help and mercy from the Gods!

They recalled stories from the Bhagavad Gita, where Lord Krishna had said that God would descend whenever unrighteousness reigned and adharma would never be tolerated:

"Paritraanya sadhunaam, Vinashayas cha dushkritam Dharm sam sthapanaya, Sambhavami yugae yugae" as the stanzas of the Gita entail.

It is believed that their worship and penance lasted 40 days. The *'Chalioh'*, as it is referred to, was rigorous: they went without new or fresh clothes, footwear, enjoyment, personal adornment, shaving, etc.

Washing their clothes day after day, with prayers and imploring Devta for succour, they heard a divine voice on the fortieth day, that proclaimed that 'He' would be born to Maata Devaki!

Overjoyed, the Hindus henceforth celebrated the fortieth day of the Chalioh.

Mirkshah sceptically accepted, though he never believed in such a possibility.

Once the Hindus knew that Devaki Maata had conceived, they rejoiced and celebrated that day 'Assu', the new moon day of the Assu (Ashwin Month).

As Hindus follow a Lunar calendar, there are 12 Lunar months for the year, so the days are less than 365; hence the intercalary month gets added every third year.

Once again, after three months, there was prayer and penance in the month of Pohi Chand (or the month of Paush) to *Darya Shah, Varuna, or the Water God*, to remind Him of his promise of deliverance from evil.

It is said that on the auspicious occasion of the new moon in 'Chaitra' (the first day of the first month of the Sindhi Calendar), called *'Cheti Chand'*, the baby was born! Dark clouds in the sky heralded rain, the Sindhu was flowing full, and they saw a venerable figure riding the Pala fish upstream, proceeding north.

Maata Devaki performed the *'Jado'* or prayer to the Water God.

An astrologer predicted extraordinary things awaiting the child, naming him Uday Chand, while another Punjabi astrologer referred to the child as Uderolal. People of Nasarpur called him Amarlal.

It is said that during the cradling ceremony, the baby was placed in the cradle no sooner than the flower-bedecked cradle began to swing on its own!

Henceforth the baby was christened *Jhulelal*!

Some months later his mother passed away; so the father Ratanchand remarried and Jhulan was brought up by his stepmother.

Meanwhile, Mirkshah was being hounded by his coterie, which reminded him of his earlier Firmaan. So he sent his prime minister Ahiro to get him firsthand information on the child. Ahiro went across with a poisoned flower to see the baby. To his shock, the baby kicked the flower away and gave him a glimpse of an old venerable white-bearded man, then of a young man, instead of a baby!

Confused, a bewildered Ahiro bowed and begged for mercy ... and later became a disciple of Jhulelal!

Mirkshah was frightened and had strange dreams of being strangled or being confronted by an old man wielding a sword! So he simply refrained from any action against the Hindus.

Ratanchand completed all the usual requisites for the young Jhulan: whose head was tonsured, and knowledge of worldly and spiritual matters was imparted. Jhulan was sent to a Gurukul at Goraknath, where he was given the Guru mantra and a symbol, Alakh Niranjan.

His mother, however, now wanted Jhulan to earn a livelihood. So to set him up in a job, she asked him to sell boiled beans. Jhulan went to the river where he simply distributed all the beans to the poor, preached to them, and offered the rest to the river.

By afternoon a vessel filled with fine rice floated towards Jhulan! Ratanchand who began to follow his son, was soon captivated by his son's deep spiritual knowledge; he too started serving the people expecting no returns.

MirkShah was now anxious and wished to end his dilemma. He wanted to see Jhulan; so he asked Ahiro to arrange a meeting.

Ahiro, aghast at this, rushed to the River and prayed for help and guidance ... Soon, he envisioned an Old Venerable person riding the Pala fish, swimming upstream in the River Sindhu! The old man shouted that Kwaja Kizier would be found at Rohri!

Another vision of Udero riding a horse swinging a flashing sword leading a large number of troops came by!

Ahiro shared his visions with Mirkshah, who finally met Udero. Udero instructed Mirkshah that who he referred to as Allah was the same Ishwar as known to the Hindus! All beings are from that One God.

Infuriated and egged on by the nobles, Mirkshah ordered Udero's arrest!

Lo and behold! An inferno suddenly engulfed the palace and Mirkshah, and his court were trapped in the surging floodwaters of the river.

Realising his foolishness Mirkshah had the grace to accept and begged for mercy.

The Fire went out, and the floods receded.

Young Udero, who was just 11 years old, pronounced that all beings can worship whomever they wish to, as the Lord believes in Diversity and Unity with bonds of brotherhood.

Udero then outlined the details of worship:

Worship is a blend of 'Jyothi' and 'Jal' (flame and water); all can worship, calling God by any name, but they must honour the bonds of brotherhood.

Hindus must have one 'daat' (sip) of Jal, light the Jyothi (lamp) and, remember God at all times, beseech welfare for all mankind by spreading one's shawl before the Lord during prayers to receive the Lord's blessings.

Strangely, Udero's brothers did not acknowledge his spiritual strength and avoided his teachings.

So Uderolal chose his cousin Pagad to carry his message of Brotherhood and faith as a priest or thakur. Pagad was instrumental in building the

Udero Ghat near the river, near Zinda Pir, where Udero had swum upstream.

Jhulelal's followers are believed to belong to the *'Daryahi Panth' (Water God Way).*

They have 7 objects of veneration: Ring (Vero), Light (Jyothi), Kantha/Prakhar (shawl), Deg (a cooking dish), Tegh (sword), Dhokla (small drum - Damaru) usually played with one hand on both sides, and Jhari (a pitcher). These were placed on the altar and evening Panjira (prayer with 5 lines) was recited in praise of the River God.

The prayer invokes the Water God to be benign, for it is He, who turns earth green with vegetation for mankind. One must seek blessings for all mankind whenever one prays.

Sindhi Hindus celebrate New Year's Day on the birthday of Jhulelal and usually perform a procession—*Bahirana Saahib*, the symbolic worship of Uderolal.

I witnessed this lovely ceremony at the wedding of Kishore's niece, Namita!

On a large *Thaal (platter)*, an earthen vessel, the Kunhri, is placed and filled with water. The mouth is covered with an auspicious red cloth: a Shivling made of Atta, surrounded by cardamom, cloves, betelnut, sugar candy or Mishri, joss sticks or agarbathis, frankincense, garlands of rose and marigold flowers, and small lit up earthen lamps are placed all around. The idol of Uderlal riding the Pala fish is placed in the centre.

The procession is taken with the thaal carried on the head, and each devotee or *'Chheji'* performs the *'Chhej'* - a dance, wherein one rotates where one stands; then the next Chheji takes over, and the thaal thus is revered by all present!

An utterly simple and meaningful ceremony that is so very inclusive.

Strangely, Udero was only 12 when he converted MirkShah into devotion.

Mirkshah constructed a temple where both Hindus and Muslims prayed. 'Lal Saain' Mandir was built at Manoharo, near Karachi.

When he was 13, Udero performed a miracle on a barren land. He drew three lines on the ground, and people found Gold under the earth! The land owner magnanimously built a temple, *Uderolal-jo-Mandir*, in his honour; the owner and his wife became the caretakers, or *'Mujawars'*, of this temple, a centre for all!

Udero selected a place near Naraspur called 'Jhijan', where he left his mortal coils.

Both Hindus and Muslims cooperated in building a Qaba (tomb) with Dargah for Muslims and a Shrine for the Hindus.

Both communities preached love and brotherhood, with or without the idol.

Thakurs were the priests who carried out the temple duties, and devotees became the Sewaks of Jhulelal.

Earlier Sindhis had praised the 2 Lals, this was merged into one *Jhulelal*.

Runa Laila's song *Mast Qalandar* glorifies the unique bonding between the Muslim Lal Qalandar and the Hindu Jhulelal! The lyrics are heavily borrowed from the poetry of Lal Shahbaz Qalandar!

Jhulelal is considered the patron saint of the Sindhi Community. This cultural landmark continues to serve as aconnection yo heritage and tradition even today The site is still venerated and is a pilgrimage centre for Sindhis. Traditional folk songs, social and religious events, group weddings and marriages, and charity dinners are organised here. Musicians and dancers from all over Pakistan congregate to perform. Devotees offer flowers, fruits, sweets and light Jyothis in his honour.

7. Sindhi Culture

The land of Sufis, love, romance, pleasure. Sufism, once pervaded every nuance of their lifestyles, though in today's world, it is swamped by outrageous Western influences in all aspects!

Many outstanding poets of Sufi poetry and mysticism, Shah Abdul Bittal, Lal Shabaz Qalandar, Sachal Sarmast, Abdullah Shah Ghazi, and Shah Abdul Latif belonged to this area.

Rawalpindi boasts of singular religious influence, and many became *'Nanak Panthis'* following the teachings of Guru Nanak. The Guru Granth Sahib is read and studied in these Gurudwaras.

Although primarily influenced by Hindu scriptures, Sindhis celebrate Diwali, Holi, and Shivratri.

Thus the culture tends to be syncretic with Hindu Vedic and Sikh religious practices.

Interestingly Sindhi names and suffixes came by as names based on Devi and Devtas as worshipped in Vedic culture:

(list courtesy Sri Bharadwaj):

Ambema - Ambaram, Bhagwan /Bhagawati - Bhaghu/Bhaga,

Bhairav- Bherumal, Chandi Devi- Chandumal, Chaturbhuj- Chatru.

Or, based on the Stars - Nakshatra:

Asulesha - Hassior, Hasoomal, Magha - Menghi or Menghoma, Jyestha - Jethi, Jethomal, Jethanand, Mool - Muli/Moolchand, Sugna - Sugni/Sugonomal.

Sindhi surnames are modified patronymic forms and typically end with a suffix '-ani', 'Ja/Jo', or 'Potra /Pota', denoting descent from a male ancestor.

Some Sindhi communities are Sindhi Sammats, Sindhi Gujjars, Sindhi Rajputs, and Sindhi Jats. While Muslim ones are Memon, Shaikh, Khwaja.

Further with proximity to Punjab, Gujerat, and Rajasthan, the influences of those names and surnames percolated into and were assimilated into Sindhi culture. There is no hierarchy in this division of labour nor is untouchability practised.

"Yes, There is a logic behind this", says Ajit Wadhwani, a young modern writer.

"Here's a piece of information I picked up from another site, which all Sindhis and communities should know!

Unlike other Hindus of India, who have a 'gotra', Sindhis often have a 'nukh', which means roots. This is much of the reason why Hindu Sindhi surnames end in 'ani'- which means 'anshi', derived from the Sanskrit word 'ansh', which means 'descendence'.

So, if someone returned or came from Georgia, his nukh would be 'jeorus', and his surname could be coined after the family head's name (subject to change every seven generations). For example, if your family head seven generations back had the name 'Tolaram', then your surname would be TOL-ANI. The same goes for all the 'ani's' in the world.

The person may have been from Iran, Iraq, Saudi Arabia, Italy, Anatolia, Armenia, or wherever this 'ani' had been, and this is unique to Sindhi civilisation.

Another variation does exist in this norm. Many surnames of northern Sindh eg: (Shikarpur) and Multan (ancient name: Sawarawkistan) end in 'ja', eg: Ahuja, Raheja, Hinduja, etc. 'Ja' in Sindhi means 'of', so if a person belonged to the village of 'Junay', then their surname would be 'Juneja'."

Now the question arises, why is there a need to add 'ani' or 'ja' to Sindhi surnames?

It's because many Sindhis had escaped after the Mahmud Ghaznavi invasion. They were called 'Banjaras' in India, Sinti in distant European lands, and 'Sintowee' in Mongolia and China. 'Gypsy' is a term used for them frequently.

However, many Sintis awaited the end of Ghaznavid rule so that they could return. Many did return, but many were pushed westward and thus have never returned.

Those who managed to return are called 'Aaryan', a term different from the Sanskritic version 'Arya'.

Aaryan in Sindhi means those who have come back."

These tribes added 'ani' (southern Sindh) and 'ja' (northern Sindh) to their names.

Already an Indo-Iranian race, the Sindhi Hindus, once becoming Sintis in distant lands, acquired a range of cultural habits of different cultures. With many inter-cultural marriages, the fabric of the race of Sindhis varied tremendously. Different dialects in Sindh were born, and different senses of dress and accoutrement were born.

It is no wonder that the Sindhis are a good-looking race with Indo-Iranian and Indo-Saracen lineage. Men are generally tall, handsome, well-built, and fair, and women have lovely complexions and beautiful features.

8. Sindhi traditional wear

Distinctive clothing reflects their identity and heritage and are easily absorbed in todays world too.

Sindhi men and women wore Shalwar Kamiz or Kurta Pyjama ensembles '. This unique traditional apparel was worn to brave the rigours of the climate.

Women also donned Ghagra Cholis, before the advent of Sarees.

Sindhi culture is one of the most diverse cultures of the world, the traditional clothes of Sindhi people are various, diverse from region to region, tribe to tribe even sometimes within a tribe, it differs a bit, as much as, that clothes become a mark of identification ofone's region and tribe, especially for Sindhi women.

For Sindhi men, Sindhi style Salwar Khamis are common everyday dress these days, Sindhi Salwar/ Suthan have fewer pleats, another style of salwar is Kancha which has wide (Pancha) cuffs, which used to be worn back in time.

Sindhi Khamis are usually shorter, and before the adoption of Khamis, Sindhi men used to wear a short 'Angrakho' called *'Angelo'*, later *Sindhi Pehriyan/Pehran* (collarless Kurta tunic) tied at either side or in the centre resembling Sindhi Angelo; both Angelo and Pehriyan were sometimes embroidered with Sindhi *'Bhart'* (embroideries) and mirrorwork.

Sindhi men also wear embroidered vests (Ganji) under the Khamis. Some Muslim men in rural areas wear a Sindhi lungi called *"Godd"*, whereas Hindus wear a Dhoti or Treto and a long Jama.

Sindhi men wore Sindhi *patko or pagg (turban)*, and youngsters wore Sindhi caps skull hugging with a distinctive V cut in the centre, embroidered with mirror-work or Susi-work. Shawls like Ajrak, Lungee (silk, cotton, and wool-made shawls), or any other locally made shawls or handkerchiefs were carried on shoulders.

These were taken abroad by the Sindhiwarkis—perhaps the first exports to Afghanistan, Balochistan, Armenia, Turkey, etc!

9. Music

In such a scenario the 'Sinti music' of the Gypsies can be called the pure Sindhi dance and music. Islamization of Sindh further brought about Sufism, which further enhanced the culture.

10. Handicrafts

Sindhi handicrafts boast exquisite pottery, glazed tiles, lacquer work, handwoven textiles like Susi and Ajrak, and leather and straw products. Their embroidery, or Bhart, is remarkable as mirror work is integral to the embroidery. The Sindhi Topi, which has made inroads into various neighbouring states, is a favourite with men as far away as Dubai and Muscat, even Armenia and Turkey!

Courtesy -some inputs from Wikipedia; conversations with older Sindhi folk.

11. Demographics

The demographics of the Sindhi Hindus are indeed fascinating.

The two main tribes are the Soomro and Samma. The former are the descendants of the Suomro dynasty, which ruled from 970 -1351 CE, while the latter is the Samma dynasty, which ruled from 1351 to 1521 CE. Among the oldest tribes are the Charans.

Among the Sindhi Sammat and Sindhi Rajputs are the Bhuttos Kambohs, Bhattis, Bhanbros, Mahendros, Buriros, Bachos, Chohans, Lakha, Sahetas, Lohanas, Mohano, Dahars, Indhar, Chhachhar, Cachars, Dhareja, Rathores, Dakhan, Langah, Junejo, Mahars etc.

One may recognise some familiar surnames in the list even today.

Sindhi Sipahis of Rajasthan and the Sandhai Muslims of Gujerat are communities of Sindhi Rajputs settled in India after the Partition. They are closely related to Sindhi Jats who are from the Indus Delta.

The ones high in Society were the Mukhis who often gave counsel and advice and were highly respected.

Amils were the 'Munsiffs', well-read and generally practised accountancy. They were descendants of the Indo-Iranian Sindhis and Alexandrian Greeks. The word Aamil comes from 'amal' -practice. Educated and savvy, they were court accountants in the Govt of Mirs and Kalidas. In the past, they had worked for Muslim rulers and in recognition of their work often received parcels of land as recompense for their labour. Thus a new class of Jagirdars and Zamindars came into being. Highly respected and affluent.

So Aamils from Hyderabad were Hyderabadi Aamils. Some served in Khairpur, Larkhana, and Sevanh. Their descendants are referred to as Amils. However, under British rule, they were reduced to Collectors and Commissioners but were still held in repute.

Bhaibands, like the **Sahtis**, were inclined towards business and trading in the kingdoms of the Mirs. In 1843, when the British occupation came about, these Bhaibands supplied all the textiles to the British troops. The Bhaibund and Shikarpuri Sindhis had returned (Sintis) from Armenia, Turkey, and Egypt, bringing back new business skills.

The Waniya correspond to Vaishya varna; with many more like **Hyderabadi Bhaibands** (Sindhi Warki), Shikarpuris, Hatvaniya, Halwara, Thattai, Bagnari. The place where they came from was the prefix to the Bhaiband ex: Hyderabadi Bhaibands or Shikarpuri bhaibands.

Sindhi Warkis were specific traders of Sindh textiles taken overseas for trade as exports. Sindhiwarkis, on the other hand, sold and traded only in materials made in Sindh, thus becoming exporters. They established trading posts throughout the world, dealing in fabrics. They were the first exporters!

Successful tradesmen with richly dressed wives flaunting bejewelled appearances were quite common in Hyderabad.

Shikarpuris were mostly bankers and moneylenders, with shrewd business acumen. They concentrated mostly in the Middle East and correspond to the Vanyas of the Varna system. Bhaibunds were both local and Sindhiworkis.

In general, the community is cosmopolitan and transcends the caste system; they do not practise untouchability.

Bhatias (Larai) and Aroras (Riasti) correspond to Kshatriya Varna of the Hindu caste system, which is found in the Thar region of Sindh or near the borders of Punjab.

They were considered to be the descendants of Lord Krishna. They were strict vegetarians, eschewing garlic and onions in their food. Gajria, Kajria, and Parmal are subcastes.

Besides the main classes, Sahib Bijani mentions that **Chhaprus** denotes mountainous regions. Some tribes there came to be called Chhaprus and later migrated to Karachi. The Saprus of modern times have their antecedents in the Chhaprus.

Bhagnaris were generally fruit and spice merchants hailing from the northern villages of Bhag and Nari of Balochistan! Later, the Bhagnaris became Wine merchants, perhaps catering to the British—Nanomals, Popley, and Issardas are a few notable Bhagnaris. They had strict customs of marrying only within their community.

Lohanas were descendants of Luv, a scion of the Raghuvanshi Sri Ram-Kshatriyas. They were experts in Ironware, wielded iron swords, and built an Iron fort at Loh Gar, which later transmuted to Lahore!! Later, they migrated to Kutch, engaging in trading and allied business.

A few sub zaats Pokarno, Shrimalis, and Saraswats perhaps corresponded to the Brahmin varna.

The Sindhu temple at Sindhu House in Singapore distributes prayer cards for Laxmi puja each Diwali, and the cards, interestingly carry this legend:

"*Sind Saraswat Brahmin Mandal*" has an address in Vikhroli, Mumbai!

Each card features the Sanskrit Shloka 'Namasthestu Mahamaye' on Laxmi and the Laxmi Aarathi on the reverse! Sindhi Hindus worship the cards, reciting the Shloka and singing the Aarathi Bhajan!

In our Puja at Diwali this year, we also introduced the card in our veneration of Lakshmi during Diwali Puja.

Sindhi fisherfolk were Mohana, Mallah, and Med. Tribal groups like Kohlis, Bhils, Dhed, and Meghwals are all Sindhi Hindus in Sindh's southern and eastern parts.

Sindhis have no caste system, but subtle differences loosely define Zaats (castes) usually based on cultural and behavioural traits; these could have been acquired from their wide travels and places of habitation!

(The Sindhi Zaats classification, given above, is loosely based on excerpts from several authors who have touched upon the variations amongst Sindhis. Courtesy - National Library Singapore.)

An interesting article in a reputed Sindhi Magazine, 'SindhiShaan,' written by Sahib Bijani, discusses the unique system of the Sindhis, which is loosely based on the old Varna system in certain aspects.

As the families grew within the Gotra, the need arose to identify each family by name. Each family was allotted a Nukh (Name), which helped to find one another. From Nukh one knew which Gotra one belonged to.

The Sanskrit word for Nukh is Lakh, meaning Laksh which in Sindhi is pronounced Lakh, meaning to know from where one hails. Gautam Rishi's Gotra was allotted Nukh called Aver, Udech & Aaen, who were Brahmins.

Khatris and Vaishas had their own Gotras. They were also allotted Nukhs.

Advanis of Hyderabad Sind carries a Nukh named "Maghoo Khatri." Ahuja and Makhija are the names of their Nukh. One of the main features is that these divisions helped in matrimonial alliances, where alliances could be made within a particular nukh!

Source: Sindhi roots and rituals by Dayal N Harjani.

NB: it is impossible to list every variation. My research into Kishore's antecedents is an encyclopedic amount of information.

Part II

The Exodus from Sindh

The Exodus

This part is about the challenges faced by the Sindhi population following post-partition and displacement and their efforts to rebuild their lives.

British Sindh gets less attention than Punjab and Bengal, as it was never cleaved in two and also suffered less than the other two states. Communal differences did persist but never in the horrendous form that Punjab suffered. Sindh was almost under the radar.

The population demographics of the Partition days were nearly 71% Muslim, dominating the countryside, while 26% Hindus were restricted to the major cities like Hyderabad, Lahore, Rawalpindi, and Karachi. 2.1% were non-denominational tribes.

Only in the rural Tharparkar district were Hindus found occupying tracts of land. Strangely, these Hindus were not Sindhi but ethnic Kutchis and Rajasthanis, quite estranged from orthodox Hinduism, so there was the least scuffle with the Muslims there. Many of these Thari tribes remained in Pakistan after the Partition, with little pressure to emigrate.

(inputs courtesy - Google).

Sindh: The Partition that Never Happened

1. *Dr. Shyamal Kataria*
2. *Dr. Muhamed Ali*

An Abstract from Migration Letters

While Partition can indeed be viewed as a tragedy of epic proportions for anyone that has a belief in common humanity, it is undoubtedly the case that certain groups were more impacted by it than others, both materially and psychologically. Arguably, none more so than those who had their homes and material possessions fall on the 'wrong side' of the newly drawn international border. This article will focus on one such group, the Hindu Sindhis, who, unlike most other non-Muslims that fled the territories of would- be/realised Pakistan, did not have a linguistically similar destination within India to migrate to.

Indeed many Hindu Sindhis lament the fact that they lost their entire province to Pakistan. Taking this into view, this article will attempt to tackle the question of whether the partition of Sindh, along the lines implemented in certain other provinces of British India, was a legitimate option at the time to lobby for served, to quote Maulana Azad's prophetic words, as a convenient 'plaything' in the hands of those British imperialists wishing to preserve a strategic base in the subcontinent to check Soviet expansionism (Azad, 1912; Sarila, 2005: 29), and thereby in the process of removing the only conceivable gift that the British, who looted India to the point of destitution could have left behind—namely a politically unified India.

The creation of Pakistan not only resulted in the loss of approximately one-third of hitherto Indian territory, but it resulted in anywhere between fifteen and twenty million people being displaced (Keller, 1975: 19; Hassan, 2006: 12), and unknown numbers forcibly converted, raped, mutilated, and killed during the associated brutalities (Hill et al. 2008: 155). Indeed few would dispute that, in terms of scale and severity, it was the most horrendous humanitarian debacle to have struck the subcontinent since the reign of Aurangazeb.

Overall such voices to partition Sindh were fairly sporadic, lacking in forcefulness and, more importantly, any manner meticulous consideration or co-ordination, so unsurprisingly failed to achieve the critical mass of support from the wider Hindu Sindhi population or for that matter the Indian National Congress at the national level. Beyond what has been inferred thus far, one can only speculate as to the underlying reasons for why this was the case, but they probably would include one or a combination of the following factors. First, was a distinctive lack of leadership among the Hindu Sindhi population, in that they did not have anyone of the stature of a Master Tara Singh or Shyama Prasad Mukherjee to represent their interests. The prominent Hindu Sindhis a the time, such as the aforementioned Jairamdas Daulatram and Acharya Kriplani, were almost entirely Congressman with little or no ideological autonomy from the core leadership of the party so as to represent the acute concerns of the Hindu community in Sindh. Second, relate to the very genuine economic interests the community held in urban Sindh, which, both they and certain representatives from the Indian National Congress, perhaps felt could be jeopardized if a partition of the province was touted. Third, has to do with the over-estimated belief in the strength of inter-communal relations in Sindh

(Khan, 2002: 218; Aggrawal, 2002: 84), which, of course, was a huge, and frankly unforgivable, miscalculation. While it was chiefly the arrival of **Muhajir** *into Sindh, especially in Karachi, that triggered the ethnic cleansing of Hindus, Muslim Sindhis were more than complicit in performing*

that expulsion. The fourth, held by certain disgruntled persons, was the 'Nehru factor', such as his complete lack of political dexterity, such as only two months earlier agreeing to Partition, expecting Sindh to declare itself an independent Hindu majority state!

(Courtesy - Department of International Relations, University of Sharjah. skataria@sharjah. ac.ae)

Leaving one's home and hearth is most traumatic and is a great upheaval to one's life.

Many Bhaiband matriarchs foresaw the possibility of losing their life savings and lifestyles when the Quit India movement started in 1942.

They had wisely sent their young ones across the borders. It is believed they sent substantial amounts of money and jewellery through trusted travellers. Many wore belts under their garments with pockets concealing the family wealth, or all wealth was cleverly sewn under the linings of travel trunks to be taken across!

Strangely Sindhi Hindus decided to move, dreading persecution at the hands of the Muslim refugee influx. They could relate to their Sindhi Muslims, however, the huge Muslim Mujahir and Muhajir surge from other parts of India was difficult to understand and relate to. With homes being snatched away to accommodate the migrant Muslims, it was difficult to understand, what was next in store! Overnight Mansions were occupied by strangers who relegated owners to the rear,to huddle in a single room!

Mujahirs were the Muslim hordes who suddenly migrated from all over India into Pakistan in 1947.

(Muhajirs was a reference to the early Muslims who migrated from Mecca to Madina, along with Prophet Mohammed, in a migration called the Hijra a significant context of Islamic History.)

Thus, many Sindhi Hindus started on a reverse migration by train up to Ajmer and then to Bombay,(Mumbai)from where they dispersed to other cities in India. Many travelled by sea from Karachi and reached the ports of Porbandar, Veravel, Okha, and Bombay.

The *Mohinanis* must have followed one of these routes to reach safety.

The discovery that Kishore belongs to the Hyderabadi Bhaibands, whose family were also Sindhiwarkis explains how the Mohinanis have spread far and wide both East and West.

Hyderabad, the shining metropolis of Sindh, often referred to as the Paris of the South, was home to beautiful Gothic-style manors and huge 'Havelis' where the affluent Bhaibands lived on wide-spaced roads, upon which Horse-drawn carriages moved. It was a city with gardens, the epitome of elegance, culture, and taste that was reflected in its atmosphere. Temples and Sufi shrines stood cheek by jowl allowing amicable relations.

Chapter 2

Hyderabadi Bhaibands

Mohinanis of Hyderabad

A closer look at the merchant community class, the Bhaibunds, who gained prominence for their trading prowess, particularly in Hyderabad Sindh and later across the globe!

This is the story of an immigrant family, who fled from their homeland in Sindh, Pakistan during the Partition of India into Hindustan or Bharat......

Let us first visit the Mohinanis in Hyderabad, Sindh!

The founding members of this clan were Jamnabai and Tolaram Mohinani, who set up a home in Hyderabad, Sindh. Practising Hinduism with a blend of Sikh tenets, they were quite conservative in observing the prevailing customs and traditions, following the usual pattern of life.

Men went abroad while women and children stayed home until the boys were old enough to be sent abroad as Sindhiworkis.

It is believed that Tolaram went up to Japan, Hong Kong, and Malaysia for trading.

They had a brood of eight children, five boys and three girls: Jammathmal, Naraindas, Shewaram, Chandiram, and Gulabrai, the boys, and Pari, Chettah, and Savithri(Saoo), the daughters.

Among the sons:

The eldest son, Jamathmal, was married to Vishni Chugani and had seven children—three daughters and four sons, Dhuru, Lacchu, Wasiamal, Dilip, Mimmi, Hiroo, and Dhauli, respectively.

Naraindas (aged 17) married Ganga Harjani (who was only 15) and had four children: two sons and two daughters—Gobind, Kamla, Kanta, and Chatru. (Gobind, Kanta, and Chatru are in the United States, while Kamla moved to Chennai after her husband Pishu Mahbubani passed away in Kano, Nigeria.)

All four children were born in Hyderabad, Sindh. Chatru was only 2 months old when they all had to flee Hyderabad and come to Poona, India, for safety. The British divided India and gave the province of Sindh to the Muslims of Pakistan.

Ganga always kept the keys to her home in Hyderabad in the hopes of going back someday.

Naraindas was in Spain when all this happened.

Shewaram married Haribai Nagrani, of the Mukhis and had six children - three sons and three daughters.

Our protagonist Kishore is the second son, while the older brother Chandru, was already in his teens when the family fled Hyderabad. Vimla, Nirmala, and Dhanvantri are the girls, while Jairaj (Jerry) is the last of the family.

Then came Chandiram, who wed Kala Hathiramani and, sadly, had no issues. So they adopted Anil, son of GulabRai.

GulabRai, the next son, married Kamlu Kewalramani and had three children—Sheelu, Aashu, and Anil—before moving to the Philippines.

Among the daughters were Pari who was married to Naraindas Wasani and they had 4 children: Poonja, Jayant, Gitu, and Haresh. Jayant born in Hyderabad Old City, survives and is in Las Palmas, Spain.

Chetha, another daughter, married Topandas Uttamchandani of Karachi, later Pune (who had the distinction of being the first Autorickshaw driver in India). They had five children: Kishin, Gobind, Veena, Ashok, and Jyothi. Today, Kishin lives in the UK, Gobind is in Singapore, Veena is in Pune, and Jyothi is in Accra, Africa. Ashok passed away in Tenerife sometime in 2023.

The youngest daughter, Savitri (Saoo), was wedded to Vasudev Uttamchandani and lives in Pune, even today, aged 91; they had three children—Rupa, Rita, and Shri, the lone son!

Dear readers, we shall deal with the Shewaram branch of this family in detail, a little later.

How did Jamnabai deal with her family?

As a matriarch, she wielded enormous power and ensured the children were focused on their future.

In those days, 'Sasural' and 'Maike' were defined as Father's and Mother's areas - or "Thore Chaari and Sadar". Accordingly, Jamnabai decided to move homes in the Sadar area that was familiar to her! It is believed that she shifted the entire brood to the KiKi house, later the Jamna house, and later to another KiKi house.

KiKi was her nickname. Her family fondly addressed her, but she was Amma to all her grandchildren.

The Arabic influences had pervaded the household and KiKi was quite used to the hookah which she continued even after they came to India.

Cultivating a taste for wine, she added special spices, dry fruits, and mishri to the local brews for her Sindhi Daru! Truly remarkably independent and bold quite unlike her kin!

She sent the boys as Sindhiworkis to different cousins and relatives based elsewhere. Jammatmal was sent to Hong Kong, Naraindas to Spain, Gulabrai to the Phillippines, Chandiram to Bombay /Pune, and Shewaram to Malaysia Straits as early as 1935.

Chapter 3

Partition & Aftermath

Then came the Partition, and in 1947, Jamnabai had to marshal her family to move to safer environs. Choosing to travel by train with pregnant Haribai Mukhi, wife of Shewaram, son Chandiram and wife Kala, daughter Sauoo, Aunty Ganga and her children, Gobind, Kamma, Kantha, Aunty Vishni with her Dhuru, Lacchu, Hiroo, Dilip, Dauli, cramped into a small overcrowded compartment; travelling in great fear of Muslim persecution and horrors of possible killing, the family travelled from Hyderabad Sindh to Allahabad UP; thence, onwards to Bombay to be met by Shewaram and Jammatmal.

Reaching Bombay was a great feat, with the family unscathed and intact. Jamnabai preferred the safety of a smaller town, choosing Pune, which was indeed Chandiram's home. He had taken over

'Deluxe Decorators,' a firm set up by Shewaram before the latter set off for Singapore.

Shewaram escorted the clan to the Cantonment or Camp area, at Pune, to 3C South Petty Staff Lines, a bungalow with a Hall, a dining room, and three rooms, with a bit of cramped space for the family.

The small bungalow was thus home for the Mohinanis after their earlier luxurious life in Hyderabad!

Adapting to the new environs, they lived as peacefully as possible in the overcrowded space. Indian neighbours were friendly and social. But the environment was far from their elite stay in Hyderabad. The lack of privacy was a jolt! The house was always noisy with the comings and goings of varied visitors.

That was how most people and families lived after they left Hyderabad. Money was carefully spent. Amma was strict in obtaining only daily needs, though she made exceptions to the rule for her Daru, and no one could question her.

Marriages were a big project for the matriarchs. Finding suitable matches and building new relationships with the in-laws and extended family were priorities.

Meanwhile, in 1932, Tolaram was on a work trip to Burma, where he suddenly fell ill and passed away without reaching India or meeting his family.

It is believed that he had not even seen his youngest daughter Sauoo (born in 1931), who was just a baby; Shewaram had collected his father's luggage and Amma was heartbroken, yet ,surprised to find a baby layette with 'Sauoo' embroidered on it. Amma henceforth donned white clothes befitting her widowed status, demurely covering her head with the pallu. However, her indomitable spirit continued to guide the family. She did not give up on her hookah or daru either: thus at Pune, she had bootleggers organised for her supply!

Prohibition, on the sale and consumption of liquor, was in vogue; suppliers would smuggle the daru, in the inner rubber tubes of cycle tyres, wrapped around their waists, to her home!!

Carrying on family traditions was necessary and welcoming daughters-in-law or sons-in-law was on her agenda. Men needed to be educated, so she ensured that Chandru Shewaram was in a good school. Girls needed to know household arts, tailoring, embroidery, etc.

Though living in cramped spaces, hordes of relatives from Bombay and Pune would sometimes crowd in! This was a feature before family functions.

All weddings took place in Pune's only marriage hall, 'Kagazwala Hall', so several pre-marriage functions were at home! Money was spent on the brides' jewellery and the exchange of gifts with the groom's side, never on pomp and grandeur of display!

Ceremonies continued to dominate their lives.

The usual *'Sagri'*, where the groom's sisters dressed the bride, and the *'Satavaro'* or the dinner offered to the groom's side by the bride's family were all observed.

Aunty Saoo (Savithri) was married to VashdevJetmal Uttamchandani in Pune in 1951, in that wedding Hall.

Today these customs have changed vastly.

The Shewaram family left Pune in 1954 for Singapore.

Amma passed away in her sleep in 1969 or 1970. The family is hazy over the exact year of demise. It was indeed the end of an era.

Chapter 4

T. Shewaram Mohinani and his family

Shewaram and Haribai had had their first baby in Hyderabad. Cradling the baby girl, Hari was on the balcony peering down, when the baby accidentally fell to its demise.

This incident was traumatic and tragic and truly rattled poor Haribai who was besotted with her baby girl; soon Chandru came along, and all was well again with the young couple.

In the late 1930s, Shewaram was in Singapore. Chandru grew up under the supervision of Amma, his aunts, and his mother.

Shewaram and Chandiram took turns visiting their wives in Hyderabad as Musafiris to spend time with the family.

Kishore was born at the Jahangir Nursing Home (now Hospital) in Pune, much to Haribai's disappointment, as she yearned for a girl.

Chandru the fifteen-year-old, proved a handful so Amma sent him to Hong Kong to be with Jammatmal.

After a stint in Hong Kong, he came as Musafiri to Pune where he was married to Veena Nandwani; they had 3 children in due course - Mike, and Nikki the 2 boys while Kavitha was the lone girl.

Dissatisfied with Hong Kong, Chandru made his way to Japan and settled in Okinawa calling himself Ken! When Mike was of age, he joined his father in Okinawa.

Meanwhile, Shewaram and Hari had 3 more daughters. Dhanavantri, Nirmala, Vimala

Kishore started schooling at Rosie Play School followed by St Vincents' Primary School in Pune.

As a Bhaibund with Pune's safety to fall back on, Shewaram had a growing family and decided to try his luck in Singapore. His first job was at Singapore Plastics in Bras Basah Road, Singapore.

Breaking the usual rules since his grandfather's time, when women and children always stayed home while the sons were Sindhiwarkis who would keep coming in on Musafiri, Shewaram decided to bring his family to Singapore. Hari and the children—Kishore, Vimlu, Dhanu, and Nimu—boarded

'S S Rajula' from the port of Madras and made the voyage to Singapore in 1954.

Part III

Singapore

From Swamp to the Sparkle that is Singapore!

This chapter reveals the transformation of a swampy settlement to a prosperous global trading hub capturing key elements and milestones in its onward march! Majulah Singapura is the watchword signifying the Onward march to prosperity!

❖ ❖ ❖

A Historical Timeline of Singapore

Going back to pre-colonial times, before 1819, the British East India Company established a trading post led by Stamford Raffles, thus paving the way for further consolidation and occupation of the Island, changing its history!

Before 1819, the island was known as Sabana; old maps by Ptolemy reveal that it lay at the tip of the Malay Peninsula.

Historians however claim that an early Chinese traveller referred to that island as, Pu Luo Chung; an early 3rd-century transcription in Malay shows Pulau Ujong, or 'island at the end'!

In the 13th and 14th centuries, Temasek was the Javanese name. Original inhabitants were fisherfolk and pirates as the island was an outpost for the Sumatran empire of Sri Vijaya; Javanese and Chinese inscriptions allude to Tumasik, later Temasek which in Javanese comes from the word 'tasek or sea'. Towards the end of the 14th century, the ruler Sang Nila Utama called it Singapura after seeing a lion (Singham) in the forest. Rajendra Chola I, Ruler of Southern India attacked the island in 1025 and there was another raid in 1068.

The last ruler of that line was Parameswara of the Sri Vijaya Empire, who fled to Malacca, controlled by the Malacca Sultanate. In the later 15th century, it was under the Johor Sultanate, which continued until the advent of the British in 1819.

Documentary evidence exists, as St Francis Xavier dispatched letters to Goa from Temasek, while Joao de Barros described the island as having busy shipping activity!

Singapura, or Lion City, may have its origins in Rajendra Chola, or Buddhist monks who named the island 'Symbolic of power'; however, the 'Sejarah Melaya', a Malay chronicle, suggests that Prince Sang Nila Utama mistook a tiger for a lion, and the name followed!

Sir Stamford Raffles is credited with creating the modern port city of Singapore during his rule as the Resident on behalf of the East India Company, ably aided by William Farquhar and Dr John Crawford. By capitalising on the declining fortunes of the Dutch, Raffles sought economic control of the city.

As he ascended his administrative ladder, he ensured that the Penang Straits, which he had Dominion, was administered very effectively! Military conquests of adjoining territories, expansion strategies, and the invasion of Java all contributed to the further development of Singapore into a major trading outpost for the British in Southeast Asia.

In 1826 Singapore, Malacca and Penang became the British Colony of Straits Settlements. Governors were installed, and Robert Fullerton was the first governor. Singapore then became the Presidency of Bengal.

By 1932, Singapore was the centre of government for the Straits settlements.

Schools, police forces, hospitals, and Newspapers followed. The Straits Times and Singapore Journal of Commerce are the pioneers in Journalism! A new deep harbour, Keppel Harbour, was dredged; Jesuits ran St. Joseph's Institution for Boys while Raffles Girls School was already in place.

However, with World War II and the Japanese bombing in 1941, Singapore's status was under threat and in the Battle of Singapore, the British were sorely defeated.

Singapore came under Japanese occupation till 1945 and was renamed Shonan or SayonanTo (Light of the South Island).

In 1945 when Japan surrendered, once again Singapore came under the British.

(inputs courtesy Telegraph Co. UK)

Shortly thereafter the British dissolved the Straits settlements. Singapore became a Crown Colony of the British in 1946, went on to get Self-governance by 1959, and joined Malaya to form Malaysia in 1963. That association did not last long and Singapore withdrew, by becoming a Sovereign state, later, in 1965 when **'Merdeka'** came by!

Merdeka is a Malay word that means 'Independent' or 'Free'. Its origin is Sanskrit 'Maharddhika', which means wealthy, prosperous, and powerful—freedom from enslaved conditions!

Lee Kuan Yew, the founding father of Singapore, brought reforms and order to this trading hub, building on the edifice created by Stamford Raffles. It is to his credit that Singapore became a Sovereign City-State a few years later, in 1965!

As secretary-general of the People's Action Party (PAP) from 1954 to 1992, he ascended the political ladder by being an MP from Tanjong Pagar from 1955 until his death in 2015!

There was a lack of good housing and a proliferation of squatter settlements. These colonies sprang up all over, nearer the river. They were called Kampungs. Combined with the high unemployment rate, this probably led to social problems from crime, a low standard of living, and social unrest. The other issue with these squatter settlements was that they were poorly constructed, made from highly flammable materials, with flimsy roofs, or had roofs made of corrugated iron sheets with plywood walls, posing a considerable fire risk.

A prominent example is the Fire that broke out in 1961, at Bukit Ho Swee; In addition, the unhygienic surroundings due to lack of sanitation, led to many infectious diseases. There was only dry sanitation, with night-soil collectors or scavengers. Further erratic disposal of waste aggravated the situation. Medical facilities were few. Traditional healer, medicine man or woman in each Kampung served to administer native medicines. At best, haphazard in each case. A midwife assisted during the birth of babies. Yet the residents of the Kampungs were free and social, friendly with no closed doors or locked entries. As Shakila recalls, nostalgically of her childhood, children moved freely between unlocked homes.

The intermingling of races happened often, too. Her grandfather from Kerala wed a Chinese woman when his first wife passed away. She thus has IndoChinese kin besides her Indian ones.

It was indeed a wonder to visit the last Kampong at Lorong Buangkok in Singapore. A quaint village setting still exists surrounded by glitzy modern sky scrapers, which I had visited in Nov 2023.

The Housing Development Board set up in 1960, before independence was successful under Lim Kim San. Huge building projects, such as 'HDB' apartments, sprang up to provide cheap, affordable public housing to resettle squatters, removing a serious social problem. 25,000 flats were built in the first two years. It was remarkable that, within a decade, most of the population had been successfully housed in HDB apartments. The seemingly impossible success was due to the determination of the government, the large budget allocations, and efforts to eliminate official red-tapism and corruption.

In 1968, the Central Provident Fund (CPF) Housing Scheme was introduced so that residents could use their CPF to buy HDB flats through small instalments. HDB flats gradually increased home ownership in Singapore.

Another problem facing Singapore was the lack of National Identity and unity among most of the population. Many people had been born in foreign lands and still showed themselves in terms of the countries of their birth, rather than as Singaporeans.

The earliest settlers were Malay Peranakens at Geylang, with an influx of Chinese; Indian labour was aplenty, indentured by the British to work in the Tin mines or rubber plantations. Thus, a multiracial hotpot was already in place, with people from Nepal, Sri Lanka, India, Pakistan, and Bangladesh making Singapore their home.

This posed the potential for problems with the loyalty and reliability of citizens and the possibility of further racial riots. To resolve the racial tension, a policy to create a National Identity through education in schools and flag-raising and lowering ceremonies were implemented.

This was reemphasised through the curriculum of "*National Education*," a compulsory programme whose main goal was to inculcate students with a sense of "National fraternity." Sinnathamby Rajaratnam's *Singapore National Pledge*, introduced in 1966, emphasises unity among the people "regardless of race, language or religion," was also a part of this.

The System of Justice and law in Singapore was overhauled, with the government implementing several measures to overcome labour unrest and disputes. Strict labour legislation was passed, which provided better protection to workers but still allowed greater productivity by permitting longer working hours and reducing holidays.

The labour movement was further combined under the National Trades Union Congress, which the government closely oversaw. By the end of the 1960s, labour strikes had significantly reduced.

Singapore took the step of nationalising companies that would not survive on their own or if they were essential as public services - SingTel and Singapore Airlines (SIA) are prominent examples. Such nationalised companies were often infrastructure or Utility concerns, companies meant to lay out services such as electricity or transport for the benefit of other companies. The extension of power infrastructure, for example, led to an increased attraction of foreign investors. Later, the government took steps to privatise these previous monopolies — SingTel and Singapore Airlines are now publicly listed, limited liability companies, even though the government is the major Stockholder.

Another major issue brought up around this time was **National Defence**. Following independence, the British defended Singapore but had announced they would be withdrawing by 1971, due to pressures at home and military commitments elsewhere in the world.

In 1965, Goh Keng Swee became Minister for the Interior and Defence, and started the formation of a national defence force, called the **Singapore Armed Forces**, which was set up by the time of the British withdrawal. The British agreed to postpone the withdrawal for half a year, but no longer. "Our army is to be engaged in the defence of the country and our people against the external aggression. We are unable to do this task today by ourselves. It is no use pretending that without the British military presence in Singapore today, the island cannot be easily over-run by any neighbouring country within a radius of 1000 miles if any of them cared to do so..." Dr Goh Keng Swee made a speech to Parliament on 23 December 1965.

This caused considerable alarm locally, particularly among those who remembered the Japanese occupation during World War II. Therefore, Singapore introduced National *Service* in 1967, which rapidly expanded the Defence force, known as the Singapore Armed Forces (SAF). Thousands of men were conscripted for at least two years of full National Service. Upon completing National Service, they would be liable for reservist duties, which meant they would continue to receive occasional military training and take up arms in times of emergency.

Singapore consulted international experts from West Germany and Israel to train and equip their armed forces. As a small country surrounded by larger neighbours, Singapore allocated a large portion of its budget, around 19%, to defence, which continues today, having the fourth largest per capita military expenditure in the world, after Israel, the United States and Kuwait.

Singapore was especially interested in Israel's model of national service, a factor in its decisive victory in the Six-Day War over its Arab neighbours in 1967. This led to the implementation of Singapore's national service programme starting in 1967. All eighteen-year-old males would have to take part in national service and train full-time for two and a half years. They would then have to return each year to update and refresh their skills and mobilise effectively.

This policy meant that Singapore could quickly mobilise enough defence forces to deter any invasion, especially against Indonesia during the 'Konfrontasi' (Confrontation) when the British withdrew in September 1971. Females were left out of national service — the explanation being that, during a time of war, they would be required to support the economy while the men were fighting. This policy is sometimes questioned as being sexist and has been discussed in the mass media several times together with the length of training involved. The creation of the national service policy is thought to aid the strengthening of national and racial ties since there is a sense of unity when training as a youth with peers of other races.

As its Premier, LKY eschewed populist policies, and insisted upon long-term social-economic reforms, and detailed planning; he championed a fierce Nationalist spirit, favoured meritocracy and multiracialism. His three important diktats were, English would be the language for all Govt. and business activities, and communication. There would be Zero tolerance for any form of Corruption. Singapore would welcome talent, skills which it lacked, from anywhere in the world, to boost its activities.

Uniting these fell to Lee Kwan Yew who, with admirable energy and foresight integrated the immigrant society to facilitate trade with different parts of the globe! LKY advocated English as the lingua franca while insisting on bilingual education and preserving ethnic identity.

Coining 'Majulah Singapora', he whipped up nationalistic fervour, to aid Singapore's onward March to singular prosperity!

Singapore Rojak

Rojak is a Malay word that means 'mixed'- a salad with vegetables, fruits, shrimp, or shrimp paste, with a spiced palm sugar dressing and a heady throw of Torch Ginger!

The flowers of Torch Ginger are an iconic edible key ingredient.

Rojak is of Javanese origin. It is commonly found in Indonesia and Malaysia. It is often served as a side dish or appetiser, and at times, it is taken as a main meal.

The Singapore Rojak is quite similar. It consists of sliced fruit and vegetables drizzled with a sweet and sour sauce of Prawn paste, sugar, and lime.

I prefer to allude to Singapore's multicultural, multi-ethnicity, with Chinese, Malay, Indian, and Arabic ingredients, as 'The Singapore Rojak'! Yet, there is a collective shared pride in being *'Singaporean'*.

Singapore was just being established and needed workers, and skilled hands in every field.

Singapore encouraged both skilled and unskilled labour.

Shewaram had been in the area since 1935 to 1939 and had worked for a firm in Singapore during the Japanese occupation of Singapore. Inspired and fired with enthusiasm that Netaji Subhas Chandra Bose ignited in him, he had volunteered for the INA (Indian National Army) founded by Bose — though this is not vouched for! He had Netaji's picture tattooed on his forearms, as a form of respect for his idol!

Shewaram Mohinani wisely decided to give his family the once-in-a-lifetime opportunity.

In retrospect, becoming Singaporeans established this branch of the family on a sure financial footing.

Chapter 2

The Migrants in Singapore

In the 19th and 20th centuries, many migrants flooded Singapore on ships that docked at Penang, Malacca, and Singapore! The journeys were arduous and perilous as well.

The earliest settlements were in core areas for their trade. The earliest ones before 1830 were at Chulia Kampung (now Chulia Street) and Market Street, where they were moneylenders and traders.

Port and railway settlements were at Tanjong Pagar, shipbuilders in Northbridge Road, textile merchants at Arab Street, naval base employees at Sembawang, and itinerant tradespeople flocked to Serangoon Road, known as Little India since 1980!

The religious temples and places of worship at Telok Ayer Street and Serangoon serve as physical reminders that early Indian settlers favoured these regions. 'Pal Kambam', 'Chunnabu Kambam', 'Kampung Rotan', 'Kampung Bahru', and 'Changpang' villages were multi-ethnic, with Malay settlers in addition to Indians.

Migrants brought languages, religions, artistic endeavours, and social and cultural norms, which were changed over time.

Today, an annual calendar of festivals and rites of passage points to the re-interpretation of the original practices.

Kishore had turned five when the call came. In 1954, mother Haribai with one-year-old Nimu, 2-year-old Dhanvanti, Vimlu, who was 4 and a half, and Kishore, who was 6 years old, once again took a train to Madras from Pune.

It is likely that Haribai's relatives, from her Maike, had settled in Madras and helped this young family board the steamship SS Rajula to take them to their father across the ocean, to Singapore in 1954 or 1955. The year is unclear as oral information tends to vary among the siblings!

The SS Rajula ran fortnightly trips from Madras or Nagapattinam ports, to the Malacca Straits, through their 'Straits Service', to Penang, Port Klang and Singapore, from 1926 to 1972; run by the British India Steam Navigation Company. It had 37 First-class, 137 Second-class, and 426 berthed deck passengers, as well as 1300 unberthed deck passengers. There were bunks on the ship with meals or one could take bunks without meals.

There was enormous space for Cargo shipments. Owned by the British India Steam Navigation Company Ltd., it was sold to the Shipping Corporation of India in 1970 and renamed Rangat. In 1974 the ship was scrapped, and its glorious run thus ended.

Originally, the ship was a troop carrier during World War II. Indian soldiers were ferried along with evacuees, and war wounded. Later, large number of plantation workers, coolies - mostly Tamils and Malayalis from Kerala, indentured labourers, boarded, to find their fortunes in Malaya and Singapore.

The trip took about six to seven days, and due to cyclonic weather, it was often beset with tumultuous waves that dampened the travellers' meagre possessions.

The deck passengers had the roughest sail as they were exposed to the elements; perhaps the labourers were those accommodated thus.

The only advantage was that the travellers could carry more baggage.

SS Teesta, State of Madras, SS Jalgopal, and later SS Chidambaram also plied from Indian ports of Madras and Nagapattinam with imports of gunnies, opium, textiles and Saltpetre.

At Singapore, the ship docked mid-sea, away from the shallows; Passengers were ferried to the shore, by boats; luggage was carried as head-loads by coolies who walked in the shallows.

Many in Singapore recall having sailed on the Rajula to Singapore. It was an opportunity for children to mix with other children who were on board, like them.

An experience that only Kishore remembers very faintly, as the others were too young.

At Singapore and Malaya, Quarantine stations operated, where all travellers were subjected to health checks to confirm that they were disease-free and to allow them to recover from the hardships of their sea voyage.

Chapter 3

The Indian Influence

The prevalence of early Hindu and Buddhist connections in Singapore made it easy for the migrants to blend in. All these had existed for over 2000 years, with Buddhist cultural centres dispersed all over SE Asia. Angkor Wat has verses of the Ramayana painted on entire internal walls—from the 3rd Century BC to the CE. Sanskrit inscriptions at Vo Canh in Vietnam refer to Valmiki Ramayana, while 5th-century BC rock inscriptions mention Vishnu. Indian concepts of politics, philosophy, religion, language, aesthetics, classical arts and architecture were selectively adapted to SE Asia.

Indian literary traditions and Chinese Buddhist scholarly works on the Buddha gained currency and our Indian epics, the Ramayana and the Mahabharata, remain popular in the region even today!

Early connections and contact from the 1st century CE to the 19th century continued through trades, monks, political emissaries, and missionaries. Evidence of these connections in distinct aspects of life, such as art, architecture, food, ritual, and worship, continues today.

In addition to these Hindu and Buddhist influences, the maritime trade routes brought Christian and Islamic influences from far-off Arabia, Yemen, to Southeast Asia.

The Pallavas, Cholas, and Pala periods of South India had deep connections with Central Java, Funan, Champa, Khmer, and, notably, the Sri Vijaya empire. All these had continued during the Malacca Sultanates; Tamil and Gujerati merchants were active in political establishments at Johor, Malacca. The Tamils were often engaged by Malay Sultans as political and economic advisors!

After World War II, anti-Malay feelings rose as The Malacca Straits agreement fell through in 1963. The possibility of a war in Malaya made the British Colonial administration prepare the locals for any such eventuality. Subtle familiarisations of air raids, sirens, basic civil defence skills, population screening, and locals' recruitment into the military began. All non-military personnel had to carry Identity cards. This allowed the administration to screen for spies. The ID has come to stay and today everyone has a Personal Identity card and number! Even long-term visit pass holders like me have a card and assigned number!

❖ ❖ ❖

Chapter 4

Mohinanis in Singapore

------◆◆------

This is a spotlight on the Bhaibund family's first challenges and later successes in a new alien land!

So, a new world was opening to this migrant Bhaibund fledgling family after their quarantine.

On terra firma, the fledgling Mohinani family was united with their father who took them perhaps on Trishaws, to their one-room apartment at Bras Basah Road.

The kitchen, bathroom, and toilets were common to all the residents! Other families, Tamils and Malays, occupied other rooms. Each family had only its room for privacy. This is how the first migrants lived, seeking an existence with hope and faith in their capabilities.

During their stay at Bras Basah, an accident shook the family. Young Dhanvantri was run over (whilst on a stroll with Nimu) - when the children, 6 and 5, hand-in-hand, were blissfully crossing the road, to see the posters at the Cathay Theatre!

Haribai was tremendously upset and, in her abject paranoia, forbade Nimu from going anywhere, even denying her schooling for a while.

In 1957, Jairaj was born, and the children were besotted with the younger brother. Haribai believed it to be bad luck to have a son after 3 girls according to some superstitious lore.

The loss of the Dhanu was devastating.

The family was now a unit and happy together. Shewaram, however, had a tough time managing the income to feed his family. He took to crafting tinsel garlands before Diwali, which he would sell to other shops for decoration. Moonlighting as an itinerant wedding hall decorator, he would take on such assignments, and Kishore was often drafted to help.

Every year, Shewaram managed to retrieve Haribai's jewellery from the pawnbrokers in time for the festive season, and once festivities were over, it would be pawned again.

Fond of cards and a drink or two, Shewaram enjoyed his evenings with his friends, playing Rummy, which he was good at. He won several tournaments at the Singapore Recreation Club at the Padang and at Sindhu House on Mountbatten Road, where he was known as a man of few words.

Haribai did not like his drinking habit, so she quietly diluted the alcohol in the bottle! In a fit of anger, he simply threw the bottle with such force that it left a stain on the wall! Kishore loves to tell this story!!

Shewaram, meanwhile, set up his own business, 'Malayan Plastics', on Coleman Street, to manufacture sign boards. He then moved the family to 1A Campbell Lane, atop the UCO bank, to a first-floor apartment.

On the second floor was another Sindhi family, Ganshyamdas Khiatiani, whose children are still very close to the Mohinanis! Gitu, Kantha, Prem and Vandana.

Prem needs special mention as he is remarkably close to Kishore and has taken to Gayti and me in a big way, too. He and his wife Naina are wonderful, friendly souls, and his son Dr Dheeraj Khaitiani is such a friendly Doctor—more like a family member— always ready to help, even at midnight!

The landlord lived on the topmost floor. He was a Punjabi Muslim with two children, Farida and Sulaiman, who were friends of the Mohinani children. He owned an Attar shop along Serangoon Road.

Today, this entire building houses the famous Jyothi stores. The owner of Jyothi Stores was once a flower vendor, selling flowers from his cart! This is another fantastic story of very poor to very rich!

Perpendicular to Campbell Lane was a small street where 'Congee' shops were run by Tamils, the Chinese sold Kueh (cake), Malays served RotiPratas (parathas), Rice etc. Nimu and Vimlu would peer over their balcony to watch the chai-coffee wallahs. These vendors would often call out to the children! That lane led to the Tekka Market. The children had a roof over their heads, were together, and life was handing out returns in a slow yet steady manner. They were happy at home with their new surroundings and friendly neighbourhood.

Kishore recalls that the senior Mustafa would ply his cart loaded with textiles, and his son Mustaq would saunter along. Even today, at the famous 'Mustafa Centre', one of Singapore's most prominent and well-known stores, Kishore often bumps into his old pal Mustaq. That is indeed a terrific rags-to-riches story, for the poor Muslim family from Keelakarai, Tirunelveli, very close to Rameshwaram. Their main occupation was Pearl fisheries.

Today, 'Mustafas' is spread over three blocks, with huge buildings where one can pick up anything and everything. Their inventory is mind-boggling and overwhelming!!

Staffed mostly by a Muslim contingent of young men and women, it is indeed a beacon of hope for the owner's brethren from the remote villages of Tirunelveli, South India; a genuinely great service that Mustafa has provided, one of generosity and benevolence in caring for those less fortunate.

Kishore's education was initially at Winsted Primary School, followed by Monks Hill Secondary, where he completed his O-levels; however, his grades could not get him to university, so he had to find employment! Kishore's tales about growing up 'poor' are peppered with funny stories about how he would save half his bus fare of 10 cents by walking back from school instead of riding the bus. With the saved 5 cents, he could buy himself a stick of satay and unlimited cucumber and rice cake (lontong)! Or, how Vimlu and he only spent half the cents given to them by their mother to buy oil for the lamps at the temple. They'd use the leftover cents to buy themselves sweets from the general store.

Once the family moved to Joo Chiat Place, their social circle expanded, and Kishore met and made many new friends, some of whom became his dearest friends. Ramesh Kripalani (Pancho), Kishan, Nanik & Sarla, Bhaga, Jasothi, Chandru (Dax), Lachh, and her sister were all among the youngsters who spent time together. Kishore's witty one-liners, PJs, and jokes made him feel like a conversation star!

Vimlu and Nimu started at Raffles Girls Primary School, and Vimlu continued to Raffles Girls Secondary School, while Nimu went to Kim Kiat Secondary Vocational School. JaiRaj (Jerry) attended Joo Avenue School and later St Joseph's. He, too, did not attempt University.

National service was mandatory, so young Kishore was drafted. He was in the very first batch. He was trained in the Vigilante Corps, and one of his duties was patrolling the road at Istana, armed with a huge torch! Kishore belongs to the Pioneer Generation of Migrants into Singapore, which bestows him several special subsidies from the government.

Amusing references to being Lee Kuan Yews' house guard, often seep through in his conversations!

Kishore joined 'Mulchands', one of the most prominent tourist shops, where huge cars and many European and American customers would swing by.

As a salesman, young Kishore's fascination for all things American simply filtered in. He was captivated by the young American and foreign women who waltzed in and out!

Three years later, Kishore, around 19/20 years old, accompanied his boss on SS Centaur to Perth, Australia. This was his first trip to a different world of various Western customs, habits, dress, and accoutrement! A fad of wearing Hats crept in, and even today, he is only fully attired with a hat!

Phew! The fad has indeed turned into an obsession. Given his penchant, the collection simply grows!!! We have hats of every kind stored in boxes in the cupboards above our closets!

Soon after, he met Anthony John Pike, a British-born Australian who was a Jack of all Trades! Born in England in 1934, Tony Pike chose Australian citizenship. After stints in the British Navy and Merchant Navy, he turned to Millinery, Yachting, and business. He later landed in Ibiza, Spain, and became a hotelier, opening the 'Pikes Hotel', which he is remembered for.

Pike's colourful life triumphed in a hedonistic culture, evoking a dream life that only few can ever achieve. Suited, booted, and hatted, Pike was a dashing hero to Kishore, who strove to emulate him!

Pike was dubbed the Hugh Hefner of Ibiza, who epitomised a 'Lifestyle of the Rich and Famous', creating a paradise for demimondes and celebrities! It is said that the likes of Tony Curtis, Jon Bon Jovi, Freddie Mercury, Wham, Spanish idol Julio Iglesias, etc., frequented 'Pikes' in Ibiza as it was a magnet for escorts, debauchery for rock stars, and wannabes from all over the world. Struggling with HIV, and later skin and prostate cancer, Pike died at Ibiza in 2019.

(courtesy: Washington Post, Wikipedia, Facebook posts of Pikes- Ibiza).

Kishore, on the threshold of manhood, very innocent and naive, in such company, fell prey to the lure of the seductive charms of this vibrant flamboyant! Fortunately, Kishore's character was not compromised into that of a rake!

A narrative of Kishore's early days captures his struggles and finally settling into business.

However, in Western music, films, habits of drinking and modelling himself after Pike in dress and deportment, Kishore's fantasy life was on!

Pike was also the agent for the UK company that manufactured sign boards with moving texts (Movitex).

Pike took it upon himself to tell Kishore that he was savvy enough to cease working under a boss and instead join his father and develop his father's business!

On his return from Australia, Kishore quit Mulchands, much to his parents' chagrin. He had lost a steady income of $160, which included a $6 transport allowance, besides the free lunch! This was tough on the family that was struggling to make ends meet.

Entering his father's business of Signboards, after conversations with Tony Pike (a regular visitor to their home in Campbell Lane), Kishore had a head full of brimming ideas. Still, he was crippled by want of funds to expand.

Shewaram had started a company called 'T.Shewaram' when he took on the distributorship for the Moving text signboards made in the UK 'Movitex & Movigraphs'.

He simply sat at a desk at his friend Kushi's shop in Robinson Road with a telephone to receive orders. When Kishore joined the business, he was asked to man the phone. There was not a single call received for over 3 days!

So, Kishore decided he would go about getting orders. As a roving salesperson, he prowled every street for shops with signage (most had signage with fixed texts).

The idea of changeable letters on the board proved interesting and unique to the new companies that had sprung up as the Island's economy rose and boomed! Soon, there were orders from Banks, Money Exchanges, new buildings needing Directory boards and any business needing signage, heralded potential clients.

Shewaram changed the company's name to Mohinani and Sons, but they soon adopted 'MOVITEX & MOVIGRAPHS' as their label.

Kishore loved to travel, so he went to Malaysia and Indonesia, which fell into his net. The business developed; he had an agent placed in Indonesia to handle local contracts. Movitex was on its way up!

Travel to the UK, Europe and the USA followed to attend International Sign Shows and meet contacts for further orders. He also visited Lagos, Nigeria, to look up his sister Vimlu and her husband Gobind.

In Malaysia, he partnered with Kamita and Mr Foo in Kuala Lumpur, with a distributor, Libraco, in Penang, and agents in Bangkok.

Indonesia cleverly copied the boards, preferring to refrain from importing from the UK via Singapore. Thus, these eventually fell through.

Kishore was determined to always 'be better' and 'do better'. He eagerly participated in courses like 'How to Win Friends and Influence People' by Dale Carnegie and 'The Alpha Course'. He was an enthusiastic member of 'SWAP' - 'Salesmen With A Purpose' and enjoyed their weekly meetings, networking, sharing, and learning from other members. As a young man in his early twenties, Kishore was sponsored by a friend Mohan Ramchand, to join the Singapore Swimming Club, which soon became a 'second home' to him. He was a daily visitor to the Gym at the club and enjoyed the spacious grounds, meeting and socialising with friends and acquaintances. His membership number is MO2!

Sindhi work culture is one of shrewdness coupled with arduous work. They go to any lengths to ensure the business is looked after, shaped, and controlled by the family. Vimlu returned to Singapore and joined the company as a receptionist, fielding calls and taking orders. Nimu worked there, too, briefly before she joined her husband at Tanjong Pinang in Indonesia. Jerry joined the company in 1979.

Shewaram had moved the family to a more spacious villa at 94 Joo Chiat Walk, where the siblings recall various special rituals their mother Haribai insisted upon. There were vegetarian and non-vegetarian days, especially as she was devout and hailed from a family with religious inclinations.

On Thursdays, she would make special Channa and serve it with Dubroti! (double roti—bread), a treat Kishore and his coterie of friends would hanker for. She also encouraged Sathya Narayan pujas and visits to Gurdwara. Kishore continued daily visits to Gurudwara until 2022 when he suddenly gave that up!

In 1980, at 31, Kishore married Pooja Daswani and moved to Still Road, to an apartment in 'Still Mansion', where both their children, Jaynt and Gitu were born. Investing in property, Kishore bought a semi-detached house at 33 Dunbar Walk and a flat at St Patrick's Garden, which was given out on rent.

Kishore and Pooja enjoyed marital life with weekend staycations and visits to nearby places such as Johor and Penang and generally lived well and happily. With the children in tow, they took part in shows at TV stations, as Kishore could easily belt out songs. It was fun being an indulgent parent and husband.

Yet relationships with the rest of the family suffered as the inevitable pull between one's nuclear family and the extended family began.

Nimu married Mohandas Motiram Raghani in 1981 at the Gurdwara in Singapore. Before joining her husband at Tanjung Pinang, Indonesia, she lived at Joo Chiat with Jerry, Dada, and Mama and worked at Movitex.

Jerry was married to Laveen in 1988, but they parted ways in 2004.

As generous as they come, Kishore had booked tickets for the whole family earlier, and they all went to the USA - sisters, spouses, and children for a great holiday doing all sorts of touristy stuff. Pictures show fun-loving Kishore singing a Beatles number in full regalia! Life was one grand treat!

Life was comfortable and all seemed well on the surface; till one afternoon, Haribai quietly decided to end her life, after a futile trip to Dunbar Walk.

She then walked from Dunbar Walk to her friend's flat, where she threw herself off the terrace to the finality of death. All the family were ignorant of her mental state and the doubts that had assailed her. This was on 3 May 1987.

An unbearable shock and tragedy for the Mohinanis in general and to Kishore in particular.

Family recalls that Kishore went into a fugue state and his whereabouts for three full days were simply not known. The tragedy had an enormous impact on him.

Things came to a head when Pooja and Kishore decided to separate; Kishore moved out of the family home in Dunbar Walk in 1992.

Dada (Shewaram) suddenly withdrew from the company, leaving Movitex to his sons, Kishore and

Jairaj. For a brief time, Chandru's son Nikki also worked at Movitex and shifted to Singapore with his new bride, Juhi.

Homebound, retired and now more of a recluse, Shewaram's health slowly declined, and he fell victim to dementia. Bedridden for a while Shewaram breathed his last in 1996.

94 Joo Chiat Walk housed the younger son Jerry, his wife Laveen and his girls, Sonia and Namita.

Chandru visited Joo Chiat once a year after Mama's passing; sometimes, his Japanese family, his wife and her children would visit with him.

The formal divorce between Kishore and Pooja came through in 1996; with the daughter Gitu staying with the mother and Jaynt with the father, siblings estranged from the other parent. This churn of family responsibilities, with son Jaynt, a teenager, shifting to St. Patrick's, caused irreparable friction! A loner, dependent on others in his life until now, was to parent an uncontrollable teenager, wild as they come! Sparks flew as the youngster experimented with hitherto forbidden alcohol, and drugs. Traumatic, tumultuous years that saw Kishore battling responsibility.

Gitu attended Raffles Girls' School and went to the USA for her Bachelor's and Master's degrees. She later met and married Nick Mehra, and they are now settled in the USA.

Chapter 5

Movitex and Movigraphs

———◆◆———

Here, we examine the family's foray into regular business practices and detail their growth, resilience, and economic contribution. This flagship business proved its presence in Singapore's commercial landscape.

Shewaram's business Movitex now was handled by Kishore and Jerry. The business of signboards was doing well, there was money coming in and life was comfortable. Soon Jerry finished high school and did not bother to try for university, instead joined the company in 1979. Jerry worked at NS Modulex, a competitor to Movietex, for a while!

Jerry brought in new clients and product information, and enticing clients of his former employer.

Soon, the World Trade Centre, On LeongKostar in Malaysia, the Central Building, the PSA warehouse, and the PSA tower in the SIA Cargo Complex were all lit up with Movietex signboards!

Around this time Gobind and Vimlu returned to Singapore from Lagos. Nimu was already at Movitex doing odd secretarial jobs when Vimlu took over. Gobind looked quite comfortable with a desk at Movitex signs with no portfolio as such.

In 1998 Kishore sold his shares in the company to Gobind! He preferred to get a share of the rentals from the factory where Movitex was housed.

Gobind managed Movitex until 2013 when he sold his share to Deepak Nandwani, known as Pete, who refused to pay Jerry. Jerry quit in 2013 and referred to him as 'Pete the Cheat' after that!

An old employee, Mr Goh, was an able supervisor who helmed the signboard business under Pete.

Part IV

Kishore Shewaram Mohinani

This is an intimate portrayal of the protagonist's character, an exploration of his values, traits, and ambitions that define him as a person.

Earlier, we saw that Kishore was born in Pune and spent his early years there in the Camp area, which holds many dear memories. Even today, Kishore loves to visit his old haunts in Pune.

Coming to Singapore to be with his father, Shewaram, was a big turning point in his life.

After his primary education at Winsted Primary School, he attended Monks Hill Secondary School, where he completed his O levels. At school, Kishore played football and rugby and was part of a band with classmates Joaquim Bob Ferrer, Sam Sassoon, Tan Ming Swee and Elias. Kishore was the 'second drummer, but his job was primarily to help carry and set up the drum set, and he rarely got to play!

The family recalls that one day, whilst on his way to a 'tea dance', he was knocked down by a lorry and admitted to hospital, where he stayed warded for several days! Kishore does not remember that incident, though he has the scars to show for it!

As a teenager, he has revealed his angst about being lonesome.

He wrote a poem when he was 17 when the family was still at No 1A Campbell Lane.

Ken S Mohinani

1A, Campbell Lane
Singapore - 8
Tel: 21495

Office
Mulchands
82-1, Bras Basah Road
Singapore 7
Tel 27824 29398

"HOME"

When'er I spend the day at home

There's no one there...I'm all alone.

The four bare walls are all I see

So home Sweet Home means naught to me.

I sit and think and think and think

Look up at my pin-up girl and wink

But she doesn't smile...darn it all

She's just a picture on the wall

My life is dull when I am at home

And that is why I like to roam

I take in this, I take in that
And when I'm through, I kiss the cat.

No one can say place is at home
I find it dull when I'm alone.

Nothing to do, I go to bed
And dream that I'm a girl instead

I wish to find one who is good
One who will cook for me my food
One who will kiss me night and day
And than from home I'll never stray

Can Monks Hill School find me one
Who'd cook for me when the day is done.
If so Home Sweet Home it soon will be
For both my sweetheart and for me.

Bachelor

Sec 4C

He was attracted to Western modes by the influence of Western movies, which he saw regularly at the Cathay cinema nearby. He was extremely impressed by artists like Elvis Presley and, even now, can sing most of the Elvis hits without missing a beat! Another passion was music, and he would sit with his sister Vimlu, eagerly listening to request shows on the radio, writing down the names of every song played, along with the name of the singer!

His purchase of an Akai M-8 Reel tape recorder inspired him to borrow records from the store and make his recordings of Nat King Cole, Ella Fitzgerald, Connie Francis, Sammy Davis Junior, Neil Sedaka and Frank Sinatra. Kishore often jokes about purchasing his first CD of Ella Fitzgerald's songs, even before he had a CD player!

Kishore hero-worshipped his very handsome older brother, Chandru, and wanted to be 'just like him.' In those days, all employees were referred to by 'Angmoh' (foreign-English names). He called himself 'Ken' Mohinani Jr., wearing his older brother Chandru's hand-me-down shirts from Okinawa that had 'KEN' monogrammed on them! His friends from those years still call him Ken, though Kishore makes a joke about it these days, saying he is more of a 'ken-not'!!

A self-taught man, Kishore was given to long walks and jogging. He was very conscious of his health. He was known for running, and one could find him running through rain or shine for hours.

In fact, one of his achievements was completing the City to Surf Marathon in Sydney, Australia!

Another quip was, he ran because girls or gangsters were chasing him! He had built a full bathroom at his workplace in Movitex and would often run to work, shower there and get ready for his workday.

An important feature was a coterie of friends who approached him for loans. Generous to a fault, he never refused his friends. Preferring not to mention names, it suffices that Gayti has a huge box file of who still owes Kishore!!

At 47, he decided to retire, enjoy himself, tour the world, and lead a gentrified life!

Pike's influence seemed to have gained some momentum. Footloose and with fancy ideas, party hopping was a favourite, as was table hopping at the club and even at restaurants!

Kishore developed an interest in Meditation and Vipassana. Over the years, he has attended the 10-day Vipassana course seven times in centres worldwide.

Dada had passed away in 1996. Son Jaynt was busy with National Service, and daughter Gitu was in far-off America. Kishore made several trips to the USA, where he loved the bustle of New York and usually stayed with his cousin Kantha at Jackson Heights! As he cheekily says, he had the 'Givenchy suite' at Kantha's (actually a pulldown sofa bed!).

Kishore met wife no. 2, Sunita Mukhi, in the late 1990s, and after a courtship of a few years, they decided to get married. Sunita took part in a competition about New York City and won a prize - which won them the 7:40 am slot to get married 'on top of the world'! CNN had organised 24 hours of weddings on the rooftop of the World Trade Centre in Manhattan on 14th February 2000. Kishore, Sunita and their entourage of friends, dressed in Indian finery, were the most colourful and exotic wedding group, and the simple ceremony was telecast live on CNN! Sadly, the marriage was short-lived, and soon after moving to Singapore, Sunita and Kishore decided to part ways.

Pain and lessons learnt from his divorces and his breakups were numerous.

Common friends had introduced Kishore to Gayti in February 2005, and they initially stayed connected over the computer! In Gayti he found the companionship, care, and affection that he looked for, yet she was fiercely independent. She was not looking to be dependent as she was a professional who could combine domesticity with her work!

After her divorce, Gayti had further qualified herself at Hong Kong University in Special Needs Teaching and helped her middle and high school girls. Though Kishore was based in Singapore, he would visit Hong Kong quite frequently.Their interest and romance deepened, and their visits culminated in the holiday in 2005 when Kishore formally proposed!

Gayti's terms were that she did not wish to come to Singapore as a dependent and would only move if she could get her entry permit on her own merit! The divorce had taught her self-reliance to an improbably high degree and given her great self-confidence.

As her family, our apprehensions of whether she would move to Australia were unfounded indeed.

Settling down to stability and contentment Kishore's life reflected a warm glow of satisfaction. and personal fulfilment.

As a mature husband, Kishore swung into the act, accepting the girls very easily.

As a postgraduate teacher with added qualifications in Special Needs Teaching, Singapore offered her Permanent Residency, and all too soon, the shift came about!

Her daughters were also offered PR. Shortly after that, citizenship followed, and she started working with Tanglin Trust School in their Learning Support department. Her older daughter, Aisha, went to the UK for her undergraduate studies, first going to the London School of Economics, where she found her vision of human geography was at odds with what was on offer. Opting out, she joined Imperial College for her undergraduate studies in Microbiology. Continuing to do her Masters in Virology and Immunology from University College London, she graduated with honours. She returned to Singapore to join A-star*, who had offered her a scholarship for her PhD! She chose Imperial College London for her PhD and became a competent scientific researcher based in Cambridge, UK. The younger daughter, Rushi, started her final years at the American school. Her bonding with Kishore has given him a cherished sense of belonging and vice versa too! In fact, for her high school graduation, I recall that Kishore helped her drape her sari with instructions via Google on her iPad! To the girls, he is Kishore Uncle or Uncle Kish!

As a family man, his influence and dedication to his new family highlight his simple wants.

Kishore and Gayti had rented a lovely, spacious flat at Nanak Mansions, where they got married soon after Gayti moved to Singapore. It was lovely with a beautiful, spiral staircase fashioned in wood that led to the bedrooms upstairs, from the roomy sitting room, bar area, and powder room on the ground floor along with the kitchen, maid's room, and bath, which were discretely tucked away to the side. Dopey's (the dog) domain was under the stairs! The French doors opened to the lawns outside where a small balcony afforded a view of the Tennis courts and swimming pool beyond!

Situated on Meyer Road where hordes of Indians lived, it was a very comfortable residence.

The only snag was that going up and down the spiral staircase, with ageing knees, soon spelt disaster!! Proximity to Katong Park was a huge attraction, as Kannan and I would go for long walks through the park's underpass and get to the East Coast Park flanking the sea! Being profoundly impressed by his mother's religious practices, Kishore became avidly interested in the Gurudwara. Daily visits to the Gurudwara were indeed the start of his day. He would walk to the Gurudwara, rain or shine. He would bring back Prasad, of wheat Halwa, in tiny canisters daily, for those at home.

Nanak Mansions, owned by a Sardar family, was sold to developers and pulled down to make way for new apartments. Sadly, the old beauty is no longer evident! A hideous box-like structure now looms opposite Makena, which we allude to privately as Fort Knox!

A sense of a family unit gradually built up. Hordes of friends, regular parties, shows, clubbing and life was full again, healing the awful scars of pain each partner had gone through earlier.

Kishore's loneliness vanished as Gayti went all out to give Kishore a stable home and food of his choice from her varied gourmet recipe collection. She, too, was equally fond of outings, parties, and friends. A companionable life full of warmth, care, and affection soon appeared. Visits, staycations, and travel were on the cards.

Their guest room had revolving doors, we quipped, as an endless stream of guests from here, there and everywhere, would drop by taking turns for an exit and an entry!

Our annual visits were enjoyable as Kishore insisted on making sure we older folk had an enjoyable time! 'Where shall we go this evening?' was Kishore's constant refrain. His quest to entertain us was paramount!

I have attended the Gurudwara, the club soirees, and even attended AlAnon meetings, that are designed to offer support to families dealing with alcoholism. Kishore's PJs are legendary. We would tease him and tell him that he would be charged a tax of $10 if he repeated a joke!

After about 6 and a half years in Nanak Mansions, they bought their present apartment on a single level at the other end of Meyer Road, Tanjong Rhu Road! It is a cosy apartment at 'Casuarina Cove'We came up to celebrate Gayti's 50th birthday and the apartment was flooded with new friends!

Jaynt bonded beautifully with Gayti with his repertoire of hilarious jokes and tales, though sessions with his Dad sometimes ended in a slanging match!

Jaynt was in and out of the house, having bought his own pad, working in a firm, and dating Karen, a lovely girl from Australia. It was Diwali, so we celebrated at his HDB flat, where he requested me to chant the stotrams and shlokas! We could light a few sparklers, too, and it was a memorable evening as Jaynt whipped out an engagement ring and proposed to Karen on that auspicious day!

In 2017 all too suddenly, soon after a visit to a wedding in Pune, Jaynt fell victim to food poisoning! On his return to Singapore, the miserable bouts of diarrhoea continued, and dear Jaynt succumbed to myocarditis, collapsing from a massive cardiac arrest in the hospital, which precipitated a coma. Kishore was unaware of the seriousness of this predicament and was hit hard, totally unaware of the possible outcomes. Sadly, Jaynt was snatched away from life after three weeks in a coma at the tender age of 39!

Shocked and with disbelief, there was a sudden letdown in spirits, as Kishore had to face the loss, a pivotal tragedy that simply overshadowed the previous sunny disposition to one of the lengthy shadows of despondency.

Suddenly, this fun-loving man shrunk to despair that was beyond monumental; parental grief is immeasurable, and one can only imagine the depths to which it affects an individual. The spectre of Depression was to haunt him.

Gamely, he did partake of Life, though visits to the hospitals and doctors now increased in frequency. Seeming lost and fumbling for words, his demeanour took on a new persona of sorts.

As his medicine quotas increased, evidence of deep depression soon showed up. Jerry took it upon himself to lend a hand by coming over to cheer Kishore. Bouts of forgetfulness came by. The onset of Oblivion, a gradual fading out of his presence, a pushback of his legacies to just mere occasional spurts of nostalgic memory; now beset with Cognitive and Neurological disorders.

The past was vivid and easily recalled, and Kishore often went into fond recall and nostalgic moments. Signs of Dementia crept in. Gayti as his anchor has been extraordinary support, keeping him on the grid.

As painful as it is to record, friends gradually dwindled. Invites to parties, soirees, and get-togethers were now a dribble, as handling or interacting with a friend who was no longer the same was perhaps a tad cumbersome. Perhaps, people were wary.

Gayti's responsibilities included her younger daughter, who was in Bali trying to set up her restaurant in Uluwatu. On one of her trips to Bali, Kishore, who was in Singapore, took the car, drove beyond usual places and parked it. He forgot where he had parked the car and returned by cab!

Neighbours helped to file police reports. Gayti was informed but needed help to do anything from Bali. The police searched for a week, drawing a blank! On her return, Gayti and her friend drove through every street all over Singapore and finally found the car perfectly safe with all its tyres intact!! That marked the end of Kishore's driving around.

Kishore preferred staying home and would venture out only with Gayti!

Alas, Gayti's professional life was beset with sudden calls. She had to quit her employment at Tanglin Trust by taking a year-long sabbatical. To keep busy, she started tutoring children with special needs, using afternoons from 2:30 p.m. to 6 p.m., as that was the time Kishore would nap and watch TV.

Five years after Jaynt's passing, Kishore was diagnosed with Colorectal Cancer requiring immediate surgery! Fortunately, the Cancer was localised and in the first stages. Beyond surgery and medication, there were no further aggressive therapies. This was when Gayti decided to reach out to Gitu, as Kishore often mused about his princess.

The spectre of Cancer drew the bonds together, and Gitu and Gayti bonded over telephone video calls. Gayti involved Gitu in decisions regarding Kishore's care, etc.

Later visits to the USA to spend time with Gitu and Nick followed, and her weekly calls helped cheer Kishore.

COVID times gave the couple a lot of time together, and Gayti handled all matters bit by bit, with Kishore's fading memory and forgetful lapses. Banking issues were hard hit. Next was his gadget usage! A computer user suddenly lost his ability to even switch on and browse. A sad predicament.

In November 2021, I came over to stay more with Kishore and Gayti rather than stay alone in

Chennai. This arrangement has since afforded Gayti some leeway to pursue her tutoring sans worry, as I would be around to oversee the arrangements at home.

I have noticed, he's given up watching CNN the whole day, and would rather spend his day with his eyes closed, either stretched out on the recliner or on his bed.In 2021, we all met up in London, UK, where my 81st birthday was ushered in; I had the privilege of having three of my four granddaughters with me when celebrating the event. The eldest, Aisha (Aishwarya), was married, and Sam (Sameer Sirohi) was introduced to me! Harsh's girls, Mandira, a doctor in the making, and Anoushka, the fledgling artist, were both there.

Kishore managed that trip well. Since then, we have made trips to Bali and Pune. Kishore is now very heavily dependent on Gayti for all other matters. Their bonds of care and affection have blossomed into a unique one. He has managed trips to the UK to see his step-grandchild Nyla (Aisha's baby). He loves the way the little one refers to him as Datuk and can hold little conversations with her, chuckling in delight.

Another trip to Bali for Namita's destination wedding! Trips, however, take a toll on him. On last year's Sri Lanka trip for Gayti's 60th Birthday, he spent most of the time in bed!

Physically, he is strong and has fallen into a routine with his attendant from Helpling, an agency that sends out trained attendants who handle the patient with empathy and care. ZarMon, a Burmese girl, comes in five days a week to care for Kishore. She escorts him on his walk, supervises his Gym activities, and monitors his daily ablutions and hygiene. It has been a very gradual acceptance of help, and Kishore has benefitted from the fitness regimen.

We hope these trips will energise him.

Postscript

Present day 2024

Today, Lacchu, daughter of Jammatmal is settled in the United States. Lacchu married Gul and had a son Sunil, who is married to Tish an American; a daughter Sonu; and another daughter. Gul passed away in Mumbai, having left his family, who he was estranged from, in the US.

Sister Dhuru's daughter Jyoti is also in the USA. Another sister, Mimi lived in Chennai for many years and raised her family there. Suresh (her son) continues to live in Chennai with his wife Sonia and son, Karan, and daughter Rekha lives in Singapore with her husband Rajan, and their children and grandchildren.

Naraindas's children, Gobind, Chathru, and Kantha are in the United States, while Kamma is in Chennai.

Chathru is married to Wendy and lives in Minneapolis, Minnesota. They visit ever so often to look up the rest of his cousins. He is an ardent and devout Christian, having converted years ago. His family has six children: Monica, Anita, Suneel, Sonia, Rajan, and Vivek. All are based in the United States.

Kishore is very fond of Kantha, her husband Kottu, and their four boys, who he used to stay with on his early trips to New York.

Pari's son Jayant was born in Hyderabad, Old City, and lives in Las Palmas, Spain.

Of Chetha's children, Kishin lives in the UK, Gobind is in Singapore, Veena is in Pune, and Jyothi is in Accra, Africa.

Gobind and Vimlu are in Singapore, and their only daughter Jaya Uttamchandani is in Mumbai and is a Sports anchor for TV channels and Media.

Sauoo with her daughter Rupa and son Shri, and their families, continue at Pune; her daughter Rita is now in Jakarta.

Of Chandru's children today, Mike is in Okinawa with his family, Nikki and Juhi, with their children Gina and Brijesh, live in Surabaya, Indonesia, and Kavitha is in Australia.

Nirmala Shewaram (Nimu) is also in Singapore. Her husband - Mohandas Motiram Raghani ran 'Mohan Textiles' at TanjungPinang - Indonesia. They were married in 1981 at Singapore Gurudwara. Sadly,

Mohandas passed away in 2010. Their girls are Dina and Lisha. Dina is a senior nurse at Alexandra Hospital, Singapore.

Lisha is married to Balakrishnan Matchap, who is a Singaporean of South Indian origin.

Jerry and Laveen's daughters — Sonya is married to Aproop Ponnada, a young man, originally from Hyderabad, Andhra Pradesh, South India, while Namita is wedded to Rivik Paul, a Bengali.

Kishore has cousins in every corner of the globe - Barbados, Las Palmas, Tenerife, Pakistan, India, the UK, and the USA.

The Mohinani Cousins group on WhatsApp is busy, and it pings incessantly, given the vast number of time zones it covers!

Conclusion and Summing up

❖

A final reflection thus allows us to sum up the unique adaptability that Sindhis have and their contributions as they journeyed across regions and generations!

The Sindhi community is generally largely cosmopolitan and transcends the caste system; they do not practice untouchability.

In modern times, the older convictions are given a go-by, as interracial and interfaith alliances are common.

Northern Sind's proximity to Punjab was the main factor in its exposure to Sikhism. Guru Nanak's teachings have filtered in, and a more modern approach to religion has taken hold among Sindhi Hindus.

Accordingly, venerating the Guru Granth Sahib, and Guru Nanak is prevalent in most Hindu households. Both Jhulelal and Nanak are venerated.

Masands are the followers of Nanak, who propagated the tenets to the Sindhi Hindus, while Thakurs are considered descendants of Jhulelal. They were deemed official 'Brahmins' of the Sindhi community and were heads of many Sindhi Tikanas and Durbars.

Nanak Panthis have a simple philosophy that embodies the spirit of Ek Onkar.

One God, Universal Love, simplicity, brotherhood, humility, equality, and tolerance, regardless of caste, religion, or gender. Sikhs believe God's will creates all humanity. Therefore, everyone needs to be treated equally and respectfully.

Sikhism advocates the regular practice of

1. **Vaand Chakko**: sharing with others, helping those in need.

2. **Kirat Karo**: earn or make a living honestly, without exploitation or deceit!

3. **Naam Japna**: Meditating on Gods Name - Wahe Guru.

One must avoid the five weaknesses that plague Mankind:

Kaam- lust, Krodh - anger, Lobh- greed, Moh- Attachment and Ahankar - conceit.

The closely allied philosophy of Jhulelal's **Darya Panthi** thus offers a smooth acceptance of Nanak's teachings.

Sindhis are shrewd business people.

"Almost a sixth sense of ability to sniff out opportunities offers them an edge over competitors like Gujerathis with their **rokda** *and Banias'- '***dhandha***' of UP, and Sindhis stand out for their Chutzpah and their* **paiso!** *They have a unique way of making money, having recreated themselves time and again; Their resilience never wavers!" says Ashok Hinduja, Chairman of Hinduja Group of Companies, in the foreword of the book 'Paiso' How Sindhis Do Business, by Maya Bhathija.*

The top Seven Business secrets *(according to Maya) are in italics for the readers' convenience.*

1. Being Money minded is good

Sindhis do not consider any work to be below their status. Whatever can fetch an income is to be pursued. We have seen this attitude earlier when T. Shewaram moonlighted as a wedding decorator or crafted tinsel garlands during festive occasions.

During the post-partition days, Sindhis never hesitated to do any work that could bring home even a tiny amount of money.

2. Sindhis believed in sacrificing profits for large turnovers

They believed the more significant the turnover, the more clients could be served, bringing in much-needed income.

3. The 'never say die attitude'

Failures did not faze the entrepreneur. They diligently made efforts, and no matter what, failures did not hamper their future steps. Perhaps their historical past and geographical shifts as "Sintis" helped them overcome any difficulties.

4. Buy and not rent

Sindhis, as a rule, tend to invest any surplus in property. That is why the community has prospered. Drilled into their psyche over generations, this habit has helped them build wealth and business.

5. Confidence backed by hard work

Lack of education and management degrees do not stand a chance when self-confidence and hard work plunge the average Sindhi into business operations that soon move to mega assets through shared strategies and planned efforts.

6. Community Pride

Sindhis have succeeded in every part of the world because of an invisible bond and kinship with their local community. Giving back to society and the country they live in helps them prosper and furthers their business.

7. Always look for the next big thing

"Sindhis do not fear to go, where no one has ever gone", especially regarding business. They are willing to try in diverse areas with no hesitation!

As Harish Fabiani, the chairman of the Madrid-headquartered Americop Group, says, *"99 grams of hard work and just 1 gram of Luck are all that is needed for Success!"*

Sindhis generally abide by their rules and bend only if it suits them. Though they fit in, they hold their own. Their word is their bond.

Home and Family are critical factors for a Sindhi. They take immense pride in their family bonds. Sharing comes naturally to the average Sindhi, though miserly attitudes are also seen between kin.

Generosity and kindness are so much part of Kishore's character that he falls prey to several exploiters! A man who can never refuse help is honour bound to Vaand Chakho, but he is often taken for granted by the others in the family.

Gayti, who is an epitome of largesse and generosity herself, their home thus affords a welcoming haven for the kin to congregate! The younger generations, in particular, find Auntie Gayti a friend, philosopher, guide, and mentor!

Kishore's love of music, both Hindustani and Western vocals, is fantastic, as his repertoire is vast! Earlier, attending every show that came to Singapore was a must. That has thinned down, as his restlessness cannot help him stay in the seat long.

Time and the Cognitive disorder have usurped his senses; the faculty of hearing now impaired, combined with eyesight problems, make him hesitate to attend a show. Fortunately, 'YouTube' on his extra-large TV helps out, and the spark of interest flares up briefly on rare companionable moments!

Plans are afoot to hold Music soirees at home at least once a week next year so that Kishore can enjoy his favourite choices.

It is my sincere hope that one views every immigrant with kindness and remember their travails and journeys that have brought them this far!

Qualities of Compassion and Empathy are essential to understand the tremendous losses, the tragedies of losing hearth and home and even one's homeland!

Chronicling this saga has been very fulfilling. I have learnt that Life's handouts are very different for each person; one should feel grateful for one's experiences and bounty.

It is a narrative that summarizes the idea that Life's handouts do test faith, devotion, resilience, and adaptability.

We have indeed come a full circle - And it is time to bid adieu to my readers on a note of positivity.

Look upon the immigrants with eyes of kindness to understand them. Berating them on their plight and misfortune, sadly,is not the way to go!

As I write, there are upheavals elsewhere in our world. Many countries are suffering similar fates... can New havens open up for another new crop of homeless immigrants? I do hope mankind will rise to better our expectations.

Bibliography

This compilation and mini biography could be possible only with excerpts from various sources, mainly books, magazines, and articles about illustrious Sindhis of yesteryears and today.

Singapore National Library is a key to the world of information my daughter had access to, as a member, allowing me to choose the books I needed to refer to.

Google and Wikipedia were my online help.

Part I Sindh

Once a part of undivided India, Sindh was an alien land of great Historical and Mystical significance to me.

1. *Historical excerpts - courtesy - Wikipedia.*

2. *Religion- courtesy Sindiyat.org.*

3. *'Sindhiyat' by Thulsidas Ahuja.(National Library Singapore).*

4. *Sindhi names- Sri. Baradwaj.*

5. *Ajit Wadwanis' article in a magazine regarding suffixes to Sindhi names every 7 generations.*

6. *Sindhi wear, culture, arts and crafts- Wikipedia; Google inputs; conversations with local Sindhis.*

Part II Exodus

1. *Exodus - Pre-Partition woes- Migration Letters -(Dept.of International Relations, University of Sharjah).skataria@sharjah.ac.ae.*

2. *Demographics-magazine Sindhi Shaan- article by Sahib Bijani.*

3. *Sindhi Nukhs, Zaats - Roots and rituals -Dayal N Harjani.*

4. *Life at Pune- Older Family members; Article by 4th generation Bhaibund-Tulsi Bhoolchand.*

Part III Singapore

1. *Historical timeline of Singapore - Wikipedia.*

2. *Merdeka - Lee Kuan Yew the Visionary - excerpts from the documentary show on Netflix, besides articles, and speeches chronicled in Google, and Wikipedia, by members of PAP. The Telegraph -UK.*

3. *Migration into Singapore SS Rajula - Indian Heritage Museum, Campbell Lane.*

4. *Details of Kampungs, early settlements - Indian Heritage Museum, and inputs from Singaporean Shakila Vasu a dear friend.*

5. *Anthony John Pike — Washington Post, Facebook, and Google posts; & Kishore's reminisces.*

Mohinanis at Singapore

Family members who shared memories, video clips:

- *Kishore Mohinani*

- *Nimu (Nirmala Raghani)*

- *Vimlu (Reena Uttamchandani)*

- *GT (Gobind Uttamchandani)*

- *Jerry (Jairaj Mohinani)*

- *Sonya & Namita (Jerry's daughters)*

- *Lisha Ragahani (Nimu's daughter) & Balakrishnan Matchap*

- *Dina Ragahani (Nimu's daughter)*

- *Jaya Uttamchandani (Vimlu & GT's daughter)*

- *Chatru Mohinani (Kishore's cousin)*

- *Rekha (Kishore's cousin)*

- *Rita —Kishore's cousin and Auntie Sauoo's, daughter.*

Gratitude and Thanks

———— ❦ ————

With a heart filled and bursting with gratitude, I acknowledge the generous hospitality, lavish attention, care, and affection I receive during my visits to Singapore. These cherished moments afford me the contentment and inspiration to chronicle this saga. A special thanks to Gayti, who once again came to my rescue, providing her invaluable editorial support! Without her patient guidance in navigating modern technology and managing my drafts, this would have been an impossible feat. A big hug and heartfelt thanks to you, dear child.

The spirit of Army camaraderie is never too far away, ready to extend a helping hand. My sincere gratitude to Capt. D.P. Ramachandran for graciously penning the Foreword, despite his demanding schedule with the Colours of Glory Foundation.

I also deeply appreciate Arun Kumar, one of my former students the acclaimed author of a brilliant trilogy on South Indian history interwoven with a captivating fictional storyline, for contributing a thoughtful Note on this book. I am indeed very astonished that Arun has established himself in many progressive fronts with his wide range of interests in practcally every arm of IT! versatile! and skilled , my heart swells with respect and pride for this young man and feel happy that once upon a time he was a keen little boy naughty and curious! A multi talented polyglot he is indeed a marvel !

To the Mohinani siblings and cousins, your valuable inputs and insights have added an enriching layer to this biography. Thank you for your generosity and enthusiasm in sharing your knowledge.

A heartfelt thanks to the artists who brought my vision for the book's covers to life. Their ability to beautifully capture the essence of this narrative has elevated its presentation to a work of art. A special thanks to Rushi , my granddaughter in Bali Indonesia, for the design of the Video Teaser for this book.

Finally, I am thankful for the innovative tools and resources that helped refine the structure, flow, and expression of this work. These modern aids ensured that the narrative resonated with authenticity and elegance.

Once again, my deepest gratitude goes to Notion Press for their continued support and expertise in making the publication of this biography possible. Their guidance and professionalism have been immensely helpful throughout the publication of the book.

Thank you

Premilla Rajan.

❖❖❖

About the Author

Premilla Rajan is an avid reader, intrepid traveller and exceptional educator. She made the jump from blogs to books with remarkable ease and writes passionately about art, history, spirituality, literature, language and learning. Her zest for life knows no bounds and has helped her transition to 21st century technological advances with aplomb and enthusiasm. Premilla shuttles between Singapore and Chennai and remains positively attuned to spirituality and a burning curiosity about life.

Credits - Gayatri Krishna & Harshvardhan Rajan

❖❖❖